S0-BTS-573

**Editorial Project Manager:**
Elizabeth Morris, Ph.D.

**Editor:**
Char-Lee L. Hill

**Editor in Chief:**
Sharon Coan, M.S. Ed.

**Creative Director:**
Elayne Roberts

**Art Coordinator:**
Cheri Macoubrie Wilson

**Cover Artist:**
Tina De Leon Macabitas

**Product Manager:**
Phil Garcia

**Imaging:**
James Edward Grace

**Publishers:**
Rachelle Cracchiolo, M.S. Ed.
Mary Dupuy Smith, M.S. Ed.

# INTERNET ACTIVITIES FOR LANGUAGE ARTS

CHALLENGING

**Author:**

Mari Lu Robbins, M.A.

***Teacher Created Materials, Inc.***
6421 Industry Way
Westminster, CA 92683
www.teachercreated.com

**ISBN-1-57690-408-3**

*©1999 Teacher Created Materials, Inc.*
Made in U.S.A.

# TABLE OF CONTENTS

# TABLE OF CONTENTS *(cont.)*

# TABLE OF CONTENTS *(cont.)*

# INTRODUCTION

Welcome to the Internet, a worldwide network of information which can be the teacher's best friend. Using the Internet you can introduce your students to a multitude of knowledge fonts, all within the confines of the classroom or the computer lab. All you need is a computer, a modem, and an Internet server to help you connect to a world of knowledge and information.

This book is based on the understanding that knowledge is power, and the modern key to obtaining knowledge is knowing how to access the information on the World Wide Web. This is true in almost any discipline or area of study, and it is particularly true in the field of English and language arts.

Through the Internet, the English teacher can help her students find within minutes what would take hours in a traditional library:

- Mythology, folklore and legends from all around the world
- Dictionaries, encyclopedia and thesauri
- World literature
- Help with grammar and punctuation
- Poetry to read
- Help with writing, from writing a sentence to writing a research paper
- Quotations
- Publishing resources for young writers
- Information on books and authors
- Biographical information
- Teaching resources, including lesson plans
- Places to have fun with words and puzzles.

This book is intended not as a curriculum, but as a menu of engrossing and learning-filled activities centered on the language arts. These activities will supplement all your own good ideas and help your students learn how to navigate the Internet in search of multiple forms of literature, the acquisition of vocabulary, and the resource guides for becoming good writers.

The activities in this book are flexible. Most may be completed by one student individually or by two or more students in a group. Many are designed for completion in one class period. Others are extended and are to be used over a period of days or weeks. You, the teacher, will be able to use them in many different ways, and you may fit them into your own schedule in the best way for you and your students.

# INTRODUCTION *(cont.)*

*Internet Activities for Language Arts* contains easy-to-use, reproducible activities to help students find and use information from the Internet. The activities range from those as simple as learning the parts of a sentence and how to write one, to writing essays and extensive research papers. It also includes many literature and poetry activities.

All information required for the completion of the activities is to be found on the Internet. Each activity includes the Uniform Resource Locator (URL) addresses needed for that activity, and except for writing activities, most activities may be completed on the activity sheet. Activities may be completed by individual students or by small groups.

---

This book is divided into these sections:

- General Information About Using the Internet
- Vocabulary Activities
- Encyclopedia Activities
- Idioms: Weird Words and Phrases
- Literature Activities
- General Literature Activities
- Grammar, Basic Writing, and Punctuation Activities
- Fiction
- Reading Poetry
- Writing Poetry
- General Writing Concerns
- Fun on the Net with Language Arts
- Language Arts Internet Sites

---

Each activity will include one or more sites to be used when completing that activity. Because Internet sites can, and frequently do, change or move, the attempt has been made to include mainly sites connected to educational and government sites, or to ones which have been constant for some time. Since high usage sometimes renders a site temporarily unavailable, more than one site has been suggested for most activities. Teacher Created Materials attempts to offset this ongoing problem by posting changes of URL's on our Web site. Check our home page at **www.teachercreated.com** for updates on this book.

If you have never surfed on the Internet, it is suggested that you read *Internet for Teachers and Parents,* published by Teacher Created Materials, Inc. to familiarize yourself with the details of using the Internet not covered in this book.

\*\*Note: At the time of this printing, all Web sites were accurate and accessible. The publishers give no guarantee as to how long these Web sites will remain online.

# NETIQUETTE AND NETHICS

Exploring the world of knowledge available on the Internet is a privilege, and like a driver's license, it is a privilege which can be taken away for breaking the rules. When using the Internet, remind students to follow these rules:

- **You're not dealing with computers; you're dealing with people.** Sending a message that is strongly critical is called a "flame." To avoid "flaming," never say anything to someone that you would not say to him or her in person. Avoid the use of sarcasm, and be careful with humor. Without body language, facial expressions and voice inflections, your remarks can be misinterpreted by others.

- **Do not post personal information about anyone.** Do not give out your home phone number or your personal address.

- **Be brief.**

- **Do not harass users.** If a person does not want you to e-mail him or her, don't.

- **Be careful of copyrights.** Do not cut or paste the writing of someone else with the purpose of selling or publishing it. It is all right to use such information for educational purposes, but always cite your references.

- **Be careful of downloads.** Some software may have been circulated illegally. Do not use it. Also, viruses may be installed in your computer by downloading attached files sent to you by e-mail from someone you do not know. If you receive such e-mail with attached files, forward it on to the appropriate authority, then delete it from your mailbox. Do not allow it into your computer system by downloading it.

---

**The Ten Commandments for Computer Ethics (Nethics)
from the Computer Ethics Institute**

1. Thou shalt not use a computer to harm other people.
2. Thou shalt not interfere with other people's computer work.
3. Thou shalt not snoop around in other people's files.
4. Thou shalt not use a computer to steal.
5. Thou shalt not use a computer to bear false witness.
6. Thou shalt not use or copy software for which you have not paid.
7. Thou shalt not use other people's computer resources without authorization.
8. Thou shalt not appropriate other people's intellectual output.
9. Thou shalt think about the social consequences of the program you write.
10. Thou shalt use a computer in ways that show consideration and respect.

---

# USING SEARCH ENGINES

Using search engines can be a blessing or a bane, depending on which one you are using and searching for. If you know how to use them, they are a blessing, for you can find almost anything you want to know with them. If you don't have much time, or if you haven't learned how to bypass the advertisements—yes, search engines have them just like television—you can waste a lot of time trying to find what you want. Fortunately, experience is a good teacher, and with use you will be able to find your way around. Go to an engine by using the URL (Uniform Resource Locator).

To use a search engine, go to the engine's page. In most cases you will find a form which allows you to type in keywords for what you wish to find. Type in the keywords, click the search button, and then wait a matter of seconds or up to a minute. A new screen will come up with a list of underlined, colored (often blue) hyperlinks. Hyperlinks are links from one document to another on which you click to reach another site. Here are some major search engines.

Inference Find! claims to be the fastest with a seven second search time, and it may be. Its responses are neatly categorized without all the extra wordage and advertising most engines have, and its selection of sites related to language arts is easy to distinguish. Sites are clearly designated as commercial or educational.

Findspot: Search Engines + : **http://www.findspot.com/**

All-In-One Search Page: **http://www.albany.net/allinone/**

Altavista: **http://altavista.digital.com**

Dogpile, the Friendly Multi-Engine Search: **http://www.dogpile.com/**

Education World where Educators Go to Learn: **http://www.education-world.com/**

Electric Library: **http://www.elibrary.com/s/geo/**

Excite: **http://www.excite.com/**

Galaxy: **http://www.einet.net**

Geocities: **http://www.geocities.com/**

HotBot: **http://www.hotbot.com/**

Inference Find!: **http://www.infind.com/**

Information Please (almanac): **http://www.infoplease.com/**

Infoseek: **http://www.infoseek.com/**

Lycos Home Page: **http://www.lycos.com/**

Northern Light Search: **http://www.northernlight.com/**

The Big Eye: **http://www.bigeye.com/bigeye1.htm**

The Mining Company: **http://home.miningco.com/**

Yahoo!: **http://www.yahoo.com/**

Post this reminder near your computer.

# SAFETY RULES FOR THE INTERNET

**Never give your online password to anyone!**

**When sending e-mail to strangers, or when posting on a message board, or when in a chat room, never give your real name!**

**When sending e-mail to strangers, or when posting on a message board, or when in a chat room, do not give your address!**

**When sending e-mail to strangers, or when posting on a message board, or when in a chat room, do not give your telephone number!**

**Do not send any credit card numbers to someone over the Internet!**

Most people using the Internet are honest and good just like you are. You can have a lot of fun writing to people you don't know. You may even become a member of a cyber community. You can learn a lot from others online.

But you need to always remember that *all you know about the stranger to whom you are writing is what that person tells you. And you never know who is listening in on your conversation.*

It's very easy to let go of caution in the excitement of writing to someone who writes back to you and with whom you build an online relationship. You begin to feel like friends. It's almost like writing in a diary, but it **isn't** writing in a diary. It's writing **to someone you don't really know!**

You can't see the person. You don't know what kind of person you're writing to or who is writing to you.

**Stay safe!**

# SAFE SURFING ON THE INTERNET

The Internet is public domain, and free speech is the rule. Almost anyone can publish almost anything on it, which means there are sometimes inappropriate materials on it, and we cannot always avoid them. While we can't always weed out all the materials which are unacceptable for educational purposes, we need to help students understand that their access to such material is also unacceptable.

Recommend to parents that they educate themselves regarding their children and the Internet. The U.S. Department of Education publishes this guide for parents, which you might point them toward.

Parents' guide to the Internet: **http://www.ed.gov/pubs/parents/internet/tips.html**

In the classroom, take some common-sense precautions regarding in-class use of the Internet. Here are some general rules.

- Maintain close supervision at all times. Circulate around the room to ensure that students are doing what they're supposed to be doing.
- Send an agreement home for parents to sign that explains the benefits and risks of Internet research.
- Make students aware of "Netiquette"—the rules of using the Internet. (See page 7)
- Teach students to be responsible users of the Internet, and suggest sites for them to visit. Set up bookmarks at appropriate sites.
- Create a list of safe Internet sites and require that students visit only those sites.
- Create your own home page with safe surfing sites on it. Customize your directory with links to Internet sites you know to be safe and educationally sound.
- Use a Net monitoring program to block out inappropriate information.
- Encourage parents of your students to spend family time Net surfing. There are many sites which would be educational and fun for families to explore together.

The following sites have programs which block inappropriate information from crossing the screens used by minors. Demonstration programs may be downloaded.

Cyberpatrol:   **http://www.cyberpatrol.com/**

Surfwatch:   **http://www1.surfwatch.com/home/**

Netnanny:   **http://www.netnanny.com/**

# CREATE A DIRECTORY OF USEFUL INTERNET SITES FOR REPORTS, ESSAYS AND REVIEWS

Bookmarks and Favorite Places are great for using when you're online. All you have to do to go where you want to go for information is click a button on your mouse, and you're there within a minute or less. But there are many times when you are working on a report, essay, or review, and you need to know the online address, called a URL (Uniform Resource Locator), for the resource you want. Your brother may be using the computer so you can't get to it, or you simply may not, for any reason, be able to go online, but you need the information to include in your paper, or to use later.

This directory is intended for you to use in such cases. It will include many useful sites, as well as space for you to record sites which you find on your own. Write the addresses of additional sites on the next page.

**How Do You Find a Site Without Knowing the URL?**

Many major URLs follow a certain logic. If you do not know one, you may try typing in the obvious.

If you think the site would be a commercial one:

Try using this: **http://www.companyname.com**

Example: **http://www.apple.com**

If you think the site would be connected with a school or university:

Try using this: **http://www.schoolname.edu**

Example: **http://www.vanderbilt.edu**

If you think the site would be a government site:

Trying using this: **http://www.governmentalagency.gov**

Example: **http://www.whitehouse.gov**

Or for another one:

Try using this: **http://www.name.net**

Remember to try different spellings of the name as well. For example, a school district may go by its initials, e.g., "ogsd" for Oak Grove School District. The initials for the state name may also be added, e.g., http://www.ogsd.ca.edu. Play around with the possibilities. You'll be surprised at how many you find this way.

# USEFUL INTERNET SITES FOR FINDING AUTHORS

Almost every author of modern or classical literature is represented by at least one page. Usually these pages include biographical material. It is impossible here to include every page or site where you can get this information, but you can probably find the author you're looking for somewhere in these lists, because each contains links to many other sites. Also go to online encyclopedia and search engines. Because each is different, try several when looking for an author. You will probably find different sources with each engine. Here are some of the major sources to help you find information about authors.

## Major Sources for Authors

Young Adult Reading: **http://www.spruceridge.com/reading/**

At this site you can find 1993, 1994, 1995, and 1996 reading lists, plus excellent search by author or title.

Children's Literature Authors and Illustrators:
**http://www.users.interport.net/~fairrosa/cl.authors.html**

Links and information on huge number of authors and illustrators of children's books are at this site.

IPL Youth Division Author Links: **http://www.ipl.org/youth/AskAuthor/AuthorLinks.html**

This site has some favorite authors of children's and young adult books, including Raold Dahl, Patricia Reilly Giff, Virginia Hamilton, and Madeleine L'Engle, from the Internet Public Library.

Wessex Author Links: **http://www.wessexbooks.com/authors.htm**

This site has author links alphabetically listed.

Author Webliography: **http://www.lib.lsu.edu/hum/authors.html**

Links to major British and American authors from Louisiana State University can be found here.

Books Online Authors: **http://www.cs.cmu.edu/bookauthors.html**

At this site from Carnegie-Mellon University you can do an alphabetical search from a huge list of authors.

The BookWire Index Author Web sites: **http://www.xs4all.nl/~pwessel/writers.html**

Go to this site for a large list of author Web sites on wide range of authors.

Children's Authors and Illustrators: **http://www.acs.ucalgary.cal/~dkbrown/authors.html**

Find here information about individual authors and illustrators

Children's Author's Search-Yahoo!:
**http://www.yahoo.com/Arts/humanities/Literature/Genres/Children_s/Authors/**

This is a search engine for children's authors

# BOOKS AND LITERATURE ONLINE

It is amazing that the full texts of many books are available for reading online, but such is the state of the information available on the Internet of today. You can find the entire King James version of the Bible, all of Shakespeare's plays and poetry, all of Edgar Allan Poe's stories and poetry, many of Dickens' books, and much, much more online. In addition to these sites, use search engines to look for what you can't find here. Each search engine will include different works, so look in more than one.

## Ideas for Sites

Online Books Page: **http://www.cs.cmu.edu/books.html**

At this site you can find a huge list of books online from Carnegie-Mellon University

My Virtual Reference Desk Books and Literature: **http://www.refdesk.com/books.html**

Here is another huge online book reference from Shakespeare to James Lee Burke.

The BookWire Reading Room: **http://www.bookwire.com/links/readingroom/readingroom.html**

Find here electronic fiction, nonfiction/reference, children's books, plus additional resources.

The Internet Classics Archive: **http://classics.mit.edu/index.html**

This is a large collection of Greek, Roman, Chinese, and other classics from MIT.

Online Children's Stories: **http://www.acs.ucalgary.ca/~dkbrown/stories.html**

At this site you can find a wide variety of children's book and story collections from University of Calgary

Online Texts Collection: **http://www.ipl.org/reading/books/**

Over 7,000 titles by author, title or Dewey subject classification from Internet Public Library can be found here.

English Server Fiction, Novels: **http://english-server.hss.cmu.edu/fiction/novel.nclk**

Online texts of many novelists, including Willa Cather, Charles Dickens, Louisa May Alcott, Jane Austen, and Mark Twain are at this site.

Aesop's Fables Online Collections: **http://www.pacificnet.net/~johnr/aesop/**

Over 650 fables by Aesop are here waiting to be read.

Classic Short Stories: **http://www.bnl.com/shorts/**

Find here classic short stories from Europe and the United States.

King James Bible with search form: **http://estragon.uchicago.edu/Bibles/KJV.form.html**

Collected Works of Shakespeare: **http://www.gh.cs.usyd.edu.au/~matty/Shakespeare/**

Complete Shakespeare: **http://the-tech.mit.edu/Shakespeare/**

All of Shakespeare's works, including plays and poems, can be found at this site.

# USEFUL INTERNET SITES FOR MAPS

Ever need a map when you couldn't get to one? Help is on the way! When you are writing a report for social studies or history, when you want to plan a trip, or when you want to draw a map to go with the story you are writing, you can find help at one of these sites.

Mapmaker, Mapmaker, Make Me a Map: **http://loki.ur.utk.edu/ut2kids/maps/map.html**

This site is great for when you need to make a map for a report, or for when you want to invent a fictional map for a story. It will tell you how Peter Pan got to Never Never Land, how Dorothy got to the Land of Oz, and how pirates used maps to find buried treasure. Of course, it will tell you how to make a map of a real place as well.

Country Library: **http://www.tradeport**

This site will give you not only a map but all the important information on just about any country in the world, including how many people live there, what language(s) they speak, all the facts known as demographics, plus the economic situation. It will show you the country's flag and describe much of what the people do there. This is indispensable when doing a social studies or history report.

Map Collections: 1597–1988: **http://cweb2.loc.gov/ammem/gmdhtml/gmdhome.html**

This map collections site holds a fraction of the 4.5 million items that are held in the Geography and Map Division of the Library of Congress. The focus is on Americana and Cartographic treasures.

Maps On Us: **http://www.mapsonus.com**

This Web site is absolutely incredible! Type in any address in the United States complete with zip code, and within seconds you will have a map with that address clearly located on it. It also includes telephone yellow pages

Mapquest: **http://www.mapquest.com/**

This site includes an interactive atlas which will also give you the location of a street address within the U.S. Not quite as clear as Maps On Us. It also includes driving directions for trips.

Maps, Flags, Timelines: **http://members.aol.com/AACTchrOZ/maps.html**

Included at this site are maps, flags, geography, time lines, this day in history, holidays, distances, and money from around the world.

# USEFUL INTERNET SITES FOR HISTORY

Exploring Ancient World Cultures: **http://eawc.evansville.edu/index.htm**

This site explores the cultures of the Near East, India, Egypt, China, Greece, Rome, Islam, and Europe.

American Memory from the National Digital Library:
**http://lcweb2.loc.gov/ammem/ammemhome.html**

This is a changing showcase of photos from periods and groups in American history.

Middle Ages: **http://www.learner.org/exhibits/middleages/homes.html**

This excellent site about the Middle Ages by the AnnebergCPB Project discusses the role of women, the feudal society, health and medicine, homes, etc.—very comprehensive and easy to read.

African-American History Links: **http:///www.evansville.net/~jbnoland/african.htm**

Many sites are given here concerning people, places, and issues concerning African-Americans and their history in the U.S.

Hotlist: American History and Government: **http://sln.fi.edu/tfi/hotlists/government.html**

American History and Government has links to sites for women in American history, early motion pictures, Lewis and Clark, the Salem witch trials, photo collections, historical documents, the Constitution, Supreme Court decisions, and much more.

Art History Resources: **http://history.evansville.net/art.html**

This is a huge collection of sites to museums, including such topics as mythology in Western art, art images by period, etc.

Historical Maps of the US: **http://www.lib.utexas.edu/Libs/PCL/Map_collection/histus.html**

Included are maps of early Indian tribes, exploration and settlement, and territorial growth.

Odyssey Online: **http://www.cc.emory.edu/CARLOS/ODYSSEY/index.html**

This excellent site on people, mythology, daily life, death and burial, writing, and archaeology of the ancient Near East, Egypt, Greece, and Rome includes teacher resources.

NM's Creative Impulse: Renaissance: **http://history.evansville.net/renaissa.html**

At this very comprehensive site, find everything from people to places to movements in history and the arts.

U.S. Civil War Center: **http://cwc.lsu.edu/civlink.htm**

This site contains links to almost anything concerning the U.S. Civil War available on the Internet.

# ONLINE DICTIONARIES, THESAURI, AND WORD LISTS

An online dictionary or thesaurus can be a big help in a tight squeeze. Many general use dictionaries are available, such as Merriam-Webster's OnLine Dictionary and Roget's Thesaurus. Others are specialized, such as the various medical, computer, and science dictionaries and ones concerned with slang or literary terms. You should choose the most appropriate one depending on the specific word or kind of word you wish to find. In addition to the URLs below, you may be able to access a dictionary through your Internet server by using the keyword DICTIONARY.

Practice using the dictionaries below by completing these exercises.

A Web of Online Dictionaries: **http://www.bucknell.edu/~rbeard/diction.html**

One-Look Dictionaries: **http://www.onelook.com/**

Online Symbolism Dictionary:
**http://www.umich.edu/~umfandsf/symbolismproject/symbolism.html/**

Roget's Internet Thesaurus: **http://www.thesaurus.com/thesaurus/**

WWWebster Dictionary: **http://www.m-w.com/dictionary**

Merriam-Webster's Words from the Lighter Side: **http://www.m-w.com/lighter/lighter.htm**

Merriam-Webster's Words for the Wise: **http://www.m-w.com/wftw/wftw.htm**

Wordsmith: **http://www.wordsmith.org/awad/wordlist.html**

Shakespeare Glossary: **http://www.ex.ac.uk/~Pellison/revels/gloss/intro.html**

1. In which would you most likely find the definitions of your vocabulary words for Friday's test on mythology? _____

2. In which would you look for terms in Romeo and Juliet? _____

3. Where would you find a selection of synonyms for the words walk, speak, work, honesty, peace, and itinerary? _____

4. Where might you find a collection of anagrams? _____

5. Where might you find words quickly? _____

6. Where might you find metaphor, simile, and personification? _____

# USING DICTIONARIES, THESAURI, AND ENCYCLOPEDIA

**Using a dictionary or thesaurus** is usually simple. It is merely a matter of signing onto the site, typing the word, name, or phrase you wish to look up into the search bar, and clicking on the search word, which may be "Search," "Find," or "Go," depending on the site used. Then you just wait for the definition of the word, name, or phrase to pop up. As examples, here are the title pages for the WWWebster Dictionary and Roget's Internet Thesaurus.

## Merriam-Webster Online

Welcome to **Merriam-Webster OnLine** - the language center on the Web!

WWWebster Dictionary: [          ]  [ Search ]

WWWebster Thesaurus: [          ]  [ Search ]

# DICTIONARY PRACTICE—WEIRD WORDS

Use these sites to find the meanings of these strange and wonderful words.

A Web of Online Dictionaries: **http://www.bucknell.edu/~rbeard/diction.html**

WWWebster Dictionary: **http://www.m-w.com/dictionary**

1. abecedarian _____

2. tessellate _____

3. ululate _____

4. lacuna _____

5. aperture _____

6. isthmus _____

7. agglomerate _____

8. anthropophagus _____

9. ungulate _____

10. sigillography _____

11. mellifluous _____

12. obstreperous _____

13. expurgate _____

14. piliferous _____

15. hirsute _____

16. alopecia _____

17. agoraphobia _____

18. conundrum _____

**Bonus points:** Find a weird word you've never heard of before.

18

# WORD-A-DAY

The English language has been made up of many different languages over thousands of years and is very complex. This makes it an endlessly intriguing and enjoyable language to study. Using Internet dictionaries, find the following words. On a separate sheet of paper, record a brief definition for each and use the word in a sentence.

1. abrogate
2. bibliomania
3. caduceus
4. consanguinity
5. diaspora
6. dishabille
7. Falstaffian
8. groundling
9. habiliment
10. hirsute
11. indefatigability
12. jabberwocky
13. jovial
14. lachrymose
15. Lilliputian
16. Machiavellian
17. martinet
18. Micawber
19. narcissism
20. pantheism

List here the words from the above list which have their origin in literature and name the work, or works, of literature in which the word was originally used.

_____

_____

_____

_____

_____

_____

## Create a Minidictionary

Using the words above, begin a mini-dictionary of your own. Each day collect a new word to add to it. An excellent source for words is this site, which will have a new word daily plus the definition for it: **http://www.wordsmith.org/awad/wordlist.html**

Illustrate your dictionary with graphics, if you wish, either from a graphics or clip-art program you have on your computer or from a site like the following. Be sure the drawings you use are not copyrighted or that permission is given for their use. **http://www.geocities.com/SoHo/2695/links.htm**

Bonus points: Turn in your minidictionary on a floppy disk you've made.

# FUN WITH WORDS

Have you ever wondered how dictionaries began or how a word gets into one? Do dictionaries stay the same, or do they change, and if so, why? It has only been 150 years since the first American dictionary was printed. That's not very long when you consider how long the world has been here, or words themselves. Words can be a lot of fun. Answer these questions by using the sites below. You may use the back of this paper to complete your answers.

How Does a Word Get in the dictionary?: **http://www.m-w.com/about/wordin.htm**

Webster's Third New International Dictionary: **http://www.m-w.com/info/w3/w3home.htm**

Merriam-Webster's Barnhart Excerpts: **http://www.m-w.com/info/barn/barn.htm**

WWWebster Dictionary: **http://www.m-w.com/dictionary**

1. How does a word get in the dictionary? _____

   _____

2. Who was Noah Webster and what did he do that was important to us? _____

   _____

3. What are some words which were in use 150 years ago? _____

   _____

4. From where do many new words come? _____

   _____

5. Where did Noah Webster leave off? _____

   _____

6. Find "Quizzes for Whizzes." Try to guess the meanings of at least five words, and then check out what the words really mean in the dictionary. Are you surprised at the words' meanings? What are some words you found?

   _____

   _____

   _____

# ORIGINS OF WORDS IN ENGLISH

Did you ever wonder why English is such a mixed-up language? Why often there doesn't seem to be any rhyme or reason to how words are spelled? Why when you hear words in German or see French words, they sometimes have a very familiar sound or look to them? Well, if you have, you weren't alone. English is a language made up of many different languages, and the study of how that came to be is called etymology. Even the origin of your name can be traced. Do you know where?

Go to this link and find the etymologies of these first names.

Etymology of First Names: **http://www.pacificcoast.net/~muck/etym.html**

1. Jennifer _____

2. Joseph _____

3. Frank _____

4. Damon _____

5. Deborah _____

6. Madeleine _____

7. Marisa _____

8. Matthew _____

9. Wendell _____

10. Winona _____

11. Adam _____

12. Adele _____

13. Savannah _____

14. Scott _____

15. Victoria _____

16. Find the origin of your name. _____

# FIND THE ORIGINS OF THESE WORDS

Now that you've found the origins of your own name and others, find the origins of these words at this site. When you get to the site, click on Archive of Etymologies or go directly to the archive.

The Logical World of Etymology: **http://www.bay1.bjt.net/~melanie//thelogic.html**

1. boycott _____

2. cheyenne _____

3. dashboard _____

4. community _____

5. betray _____

6. cable _____

7. cornucopia _____

8. ketchup _____

9. love _____

10. thumb _____

11. witch _____

12. generation X _____

13. gossip _____

14. orange _____

15. obedience _____

16. politically correct _____

If you have a word you'd like to look up to find its origin, go to this site.
The Word Detective: **http://www.users.interport.net/~words1/**

For other sites on etymology, go to this site.
Links to Etymologically-Related Sites: **http://bay1.bjt.net/~melanie//et_links.html**

# OXYMORA

An Oxymoron is two words put together which seem to contradict each other. For example, the words "almost totally" would be an oxymoron, because something is either "almost" or it is totally." It cannot be both. You may find many oxymora at this site, and you may even be able to come up with one or two of your own. Explain in your own words why each of the below expressions is an oxymoron. You may go to a dictionary if you do not know a word.

Oxymora: **http://www.wordfocus.com/oxymora-a-f.html**

1. accurate rumors _____

2. almost safe _____

3. baby grand _____

4. bad health _____

5. bright night _____

6. clearly confused _____

7. clever fool _____

8. deafening silence _____

9. deliberate mistake _____

10. expected surprise _____

11. friendly argument _____

12. future history _____

13. pretty ugly _____

14. random order _____

15. same difference _____

16. serious humor _____

17. small crowd _____

18. stand down _____

# ENCYCLOPEDIA

Encyclopedia are books or sets of books which contain articles on many different subjects. Usually, there will be only one general article for each subject requested; however, sometimes additional articles related to the general one will be referred to along with it. Encyclopedia are most often used in such subjects as science, social science, biographies, etc., but they are also useful when doing a variety of searches on literary matters. Use the online encyclopedia below to research the following authors and find the information requested.

Encarta Online Home Encyclopedia: **http://encarta.msn.com/EncartaHome.asp**

Encyclopedia.com from Electric Library: **http://www.encyclopedia.com**

Free Internet Encyclopedia-Micro Reference: **http://www.cs.uh.edu/%7eclifton/micro.a.html**

Grolier Multimedia Encyclopedia Online: (subscription service) **http://gme.grolier.com**

**Authors:** Mark Twain, Emily Dickinson, Edgar Allan Poe, Ernest Hemingway, Daniel Defoe, John Steinbeck, Judy Blume, Harper Lee, Truman Capote, William Golding, Margaret Atwood, Pearl S. Buck, Toni Morrison, Richard Wright, Charlotte Bronte, George Eliot, Louisa May Alcott, Jane Austen

**Directions:** Using at least two different encyclopedia, record the following information on each of the above authors on a separate sheet of paper.

Author's name _____

Type of literature written by author _____

Years during which author wrote (writes) _____

List three works by author _____

_____

_____

In which two encyclopedias did you find information on this author? _____

_____

_____

How long did it take you to find this information? _____

# ENCYCLOPEDIA: LITERARY PERIODS

European and American literature is often said to belong to a certain style of writing based on its characteristics and when it was written. There are distinct differences among styles and the works written by the authors of each. Use the encyclopedia on the previous page to find the major characteristics of each style and list three or more authors who wrote in that style. You may need to look in two or three sources to find each.

**Romanticism:** Characteristics : _____

_____

    **Romantic authors:** _____

_____

**Naturalism:** Characteristics: _____

_____

    **Naturalist authors:** _____

_____

**Transcendentalism:** Characteristics:_____

_____

    **Transcendentalist authors:**_____

_____

**Realism:** Characteristics: _____

_____

    **Realistic authors:** _____

_____

**Victorian literature:** Characteristics: _____

_____

    **Victorian authors:** _____

_____

# PRACTICE FINDING INFORMATION

When writing reports, stories, and essays, you often need to find all sorts of information that does not seem to have anything to do with language arts, but which are necessary for your paper to make sense and ring true. These sites are useful for finding these various bits of information to use in your writing. Use them in situations like those below where you need to find miscellaneous information for your paper.

**Find the site which will give you the information you need and record the title and URL of the site.**

Ask Janis-Editorial and Rewrite Service: **http://www.askjanis.com/dict.htm**

My Virtual Encyclopedia: **http://www.refdesk.com/myency.html**

Information Please: **http://www.infoplease.com/**

Best Information on the Net: **http://www.sau.edu/cwis/internet/wild/index.htm**

Research It!: **http://www.itools.com/research-it/research-it.html**

1. You're writing a story about a girl in Kansas. In your story, the girl's home is on a farm, and she is outside the house when a sudden storm comes up. The storm is ferocious and she is unable to get to the house in time before the wind picks her up and carries her from the spot where she is running. She is knocked out by something flying through the air before she lands and wakes up to find herself in a magical kingdom. You need to find out what kind of storm would come up in Kansas and what time of the year such storms would occur. Find a site which would tell you such information.

Name of site _____

URL of site _____

2. In your social studies class, you have been assigned to write a current events report on a topic about which you know nothing. The topic is child labor and you are to write an essay about child labor around the world. Tell how child labor today is like or unlike the conditions of child labor during the time when Charles Dickens was writing *Oliver Twist*. You know that children of Dickens' time had to work in dark, dirty factories, that they were paid very little, and that they got sick a lot because they did not have good medical care or nutritious food, but you know nothing at all about child labor today. After all, none of the children you know work in factories, but your teacher says there are children in the world who do have to work instead of going to school as you and your friends do. To locate information on child labor in the world today, where will you go?

Name of site _____

URL of site _____

# PRACTICE FINDING INFORMATION *(cont.)*

3. You are doing research for a report on the United Nations. In your reading you find the words *du jour, beau,* and *merci beaucoups.* You are not sure whether those are real words or not because you've never heard of them before, but the site from which you've taken much of your information seems reliable. The words are in an article about France, so you think they may be French. Where can you go to find out whether they are really French words and, if they are, what they mean?

Name of site _____

URL of site _____

4. You are writing a paper about television news. Part of your assignment is to compare two major news networks and how they cover the news. You do not have a television set where you are working, so you think you might be able to find the news networks online. You think that if you can find them online, you can compare those stories the two networks are talking about right now. Are they talking about the same stories? Or does each put emphasis on a different story? Where can you go to learn how to find the two networks and their online sites?

Name of site _____

URL of site _____

5. Your school has a career center where students can explore what's involved in different careers: what education is required and what typical duties might be. You are supposed to compare two careers, and you have decided to compare the careers of teaching and computer programming. Where might you find information on those two careers?

Name of site _____

URL of site _____

## Now answer these questions:

1. Of all the sites you checked out, which was easiest to use and why?

_____

2. If you were going to set up a research site of your own, what would you include in it? You may use the back of this page for your answer.

**Note:** The following site is free, but it must be downloaded to use it.

CIA 1997 World Factbook: **http://www.odci.gov/cia/publications/factbook/index.html**

# IDIOMS: WEIRD WORDS AND PHRASES

People new to the United States often become confused by the language, even when they have studied English in their home country. When they do, it is usually because they do not understand the many idioms in the language. There are thousands of them: words, phrases and expressions which mean something different from what they seem to say. For example, a native speaker might say, "It's raining cats and dogs," meaning it's raining hard. Someone who does not understand this idiom might think the speaker was a little crazy. After all, cats and dogs do not fall from the sky, do they? Go to the following site to find the meanings of these American idioms:

The Weekly Idiom: **http://www.comenius.com/idiom/index.html**

1. drop in the bucket _____

2. above all_____

3. in the black_____

4. it beats me _____

5. the sky's the limit_____

6. on the edge of my seat_____

7. to be in hot water _____

8. to be a drag _____

9. to be out of it __ _____

10. to beat around the bush _____

11. to bend over backwards _____

12. to break the news _____

13. to call it quits _____

14. to chew the fat _____

ESL Idiom Page: **http://www.pacificnet.net/~sperling/idioms.cgi**

Idioms: Complete List: **http://www.eslcafe.com/idioms/id-list.html**

Idiom: Definitions and Examples: **http://www.eslcafe.com/idioms/id-mngs.html**

ToonIn to Idioms and Word Oddities: **http://www.elfs.com/2ninX-Title.html**

Word Oddities: **http://members.aol.com/gulfhigh2/words.html**

# ILLUSTRATE WEIRD WORDS AND PHRASES

What pictures do these sayings bring up in your mind? Using the same sites as on the previous page, find the meanings of these idioms and illustrate them.

| | | |
|---|---|---|
| 1. a spitting image | 2. sitting pretty | 3. to be head over heels |
| 4. bark up the wrong tree | 5. bite off more than one can chew | 6. bug someone |
| 7. cost an arm and a leg | 8. monkey around | 9. pull someone's leg |
| 10. pick someone's brain | 11. under the weather | 13. to ring a bell |

# LEARNING ABOUT ANNE FRANK

*Anne Frank: The Diary of a Young Girl* has, since its publication in 1952, become one of the longest-lived and most powerful of the books coming out of World War II and the Holocaust because it humanized one of the war's victims. Millions of people read it every year. In the diary, a teenaged girl wrote about having to hide in an attic with her family to save her life when she should have been going to school and parties and celebrating holidays with her family and friends in their home and community. Her story is a tragedy in every sense of the word, with one exception: none of the people who have read her diary could ever again depersonalize the many, many victims of Hitler's Germany who died, as Anne and her mother and sister did, in the horrible conditions of a concentration camp. Anne was a real person with hopes and dreams just like any other young girl. Using the sites below to find your information, answer the following questions about Anne Frank.

Anne Frank: **http://www.ncsa.uiuc.edu/edu/classroom/k12-projects/fall/anne/index.htm**

The virtual Anne Frank House + many resources/site: **http://qumran.com/anne_frank/**

Anne Frank and the Diary: **gopher://pwa.acused.edu/00/toys/Discussion/holocaust/anne.frank**

Anne Frank's Time Line: **http://www.uen.org/utahlink/lp_res/AnneFrankTimeline.html**

Who was Anne Frank? Record personal information about her: birth date, parents' names, siblings, place of residence, date and cause of death._____

_____

What was the Holocaust? _____

_____

Why is it important to remember Anne Frank and her family? _____

_____

Cite one thing Anne Frank said in her diary you thought was very astute. _____

_____

Write a letter to Anne thanking her for sharing her diary with the world.

# FICTIONAL HEROES

Anne spent a lot of her study time reading Greek and Roman mythology. It was her favorite subject, although the others in the Secret Annex thought it a little strange that a girl her age should be so fascinated with mythology. People have been reading and telling stories from the mythology of ancient Greece for over two thousand years, so Anne really was not all that strange for liking it.

Greek mythology includes stories about all the Olympian gods and goddesses in which the ancient Greeks believed. There were twelve altogether. Their names were:

| | | |
|---|---|---|
| Zeus (father of the gods) | Hephaestus | Hermes |
| Hera | Hestia | Artemis |
| Athena | Ares | Poseidon |
| Aphrodite | Apollo | Hades |

Using the sites below, find the answers to these questions about the Greek myths of which Anne was so fond.

Hellenic Pantheon: **http://www.geocities.com/Athens/Acropolis/3628/index.html**

Ancient Gods (family tree): **http://www.hol.gr/greece/ancgods.htm**

Women in Classical Mythology: **http://vanaheim.princeton,edu/Myth/**

Perseus Project: **http://www.perseus.tufts.edu/**

Ancient Gods (The Olympians): **http://www.hol.gr/greece/olymp.htm**

1. According to the ancient Greeks, what was in the beginning? _____

2. What was Zeus to Athena, Ares, and Hephaestus? _____

3. Who were the two brothers of Zeus? _____

4. After Hades and his brothers overthrew their father, they drew lots to see which part of the world each would rule. What world did Hades get? _____

5. Name the goddesses of love, the hearth, the city, and the hunt. _____

6. What were the Olympian gods named after? _____

7. Which Olympian god would you most like to meet and why? Write your answer on the back of this page.

# FAMILY TREE OF THE GREEK GODS

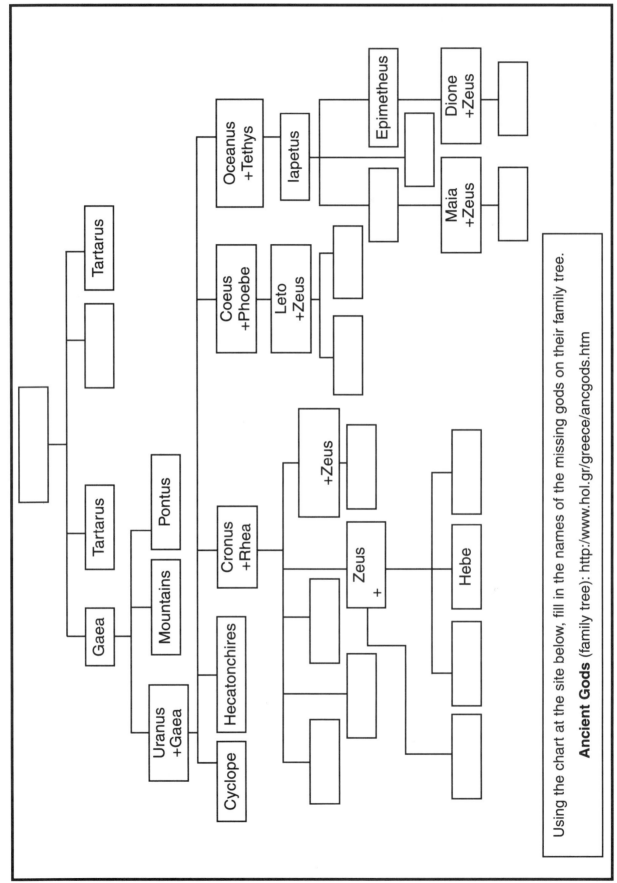

Using the chart at the site below, fill in the names of the missing gods on their family tree.

**Ancient Gods** (family tree): http://www.hol.gr/greece/ancgods.htm

# PERSONAL HEROES

Most people have heroes. Some heroes are great statesmen. Some have accomplished something important, such as a breakthrough in medicine or the invention of something which improves the quality of life. Other people deserve to be called heroes because of their immense courage in spite of personal danger, such as a firefighter who saves the lives of people in a burning building.

With some people, a terrible situation brings out the best in them and causes them to take action at great peril to themselves. Eli, Miep, and the others who brought food and news to the inhabitants of the Secret Annex, were heroes like this. They risked their own lives to try to save the lives of their friends. They became heroes who taught us the real meaning of courage.

Anne Frank was also a hero because she wrote a diary which has touched the lives of millions of people in very important ways and which continues to teach courage. No one could ever feel the same about racial or religious prejudice and discrimination after reading *Anne Frank: The Diary of a Young Girl.*

Who is your hero?_____

What qualities does this person have which you admire? _____

_____

Do you try to be like your hero? How?_____

_____

**Using the Internet** sites below, find information about a person you admire and write a two-page or longer biography of that person. Don't just copy the information you find. Rewrite it in your own words and cite your sources of information (see citing sources, page 53). **Bonus points:** Include a photograph or drawing of this person.

A&E Biography site: **http://www.biography.com/**

Inference Find (search engine): **http://www.infind.com/**

Infoseek (search engine): **http://www.infoseek.com/**

AltaVista (search engine): **http://www.altavista.com/**

Biography Maker: **http://www.bham.wednet.edu/bio/biomak2htm**

# LEARNING ABOUT HARPER LEE

*To Kill a Mockingbird* is the only book Harper Lee has published, but it has gained importance as a piece of literature. The novel is a story of injustice and prejudice in the South during the 1930s. It is also a story of the courage of one man as he was seen through the eyes of a child. Go to these sites about Harper Lee and find information about her.

Biography Harper Lee: **http://www.chebucto.ns.ca/Culture/HarperLee/bio.html**

Monroeville, The Literary Capital of Alabama: **http://www.frontiernet.net/~monroeco/**

1. Harper Lee's parents _____

2. Lee's hometown _____

3. Name two essays written by Lee _____

    _____

4. Find another famous writer from Lee's hometown _____

5. Name of the local newspaper _____

6. County motto _____

    _____

7. What was there in Harper Lee's childhood that might have influenced her to write a book about prejudice and injustice?

    _____

    _____

    _____

In *To Kill a Mockingbird,* Atticus Finch takes a very unpopular stand when he defends a black man during a time when the South was segregated. In this book, he becomes a symbol for courage and the search for justice. There have been many real-life people who have taken unpopular stands in the search for justice. Some of them have been Sojourner Truth, Chief Joseph, Mahatma Gandhi, Susan B. Anthony, and Cesar Chavez. Go to one of these encyclopedia sites, and research one of these people. Write two paragraphs about who that person was and what he or she took a stand on. Why was that stand unpopular?

Encarta Online Home Encyclopedia: **http://encarta.msn.com/EncartaHome.asp**

Encyclopedia.com from Electric Library: **http://www.encyclopedia.com**

Free Internet Encyclopedia-Micro Reference: **http://www.cs.uh.edu/%7eclifton/micro.a.html**

# SYMBOLISM IN "TO KILL A MOCKINGBIRD"

When Atticus gave Jem and Scout their air rifles, he told them, "Shoot all the bluejays you want, if you can hit 'em, but remember it's a sin to kill a mockingbird." Scout wondered. It was the only time she had heard her father say anything was a sin. When she asked Maudie what Atticus had meant, Maudie said the only thing mockingbirds do is "sing their hearts out for us," and it's wrong to kill something that does that.

This is important in several ways. For one thing, it provides the title of the book, but even more important is what the mockingbird symbolizes in the book: those things and people who give pleasure and do good for others. The most obvious people symbolized by the mockingbird are Tom Robinson, who helps even the poor, ignorant girl who abuses his good nature and good heart—and dies for it, and Boo Radley, who in his own quiet, reclusive way gives pleasure to the children by leaving small surprises for them where they can find them.

Any good piece of literature has such symbols: things which represent ideas and enhance the story's meaning. Here are some common symbols used in literature. Find and list the symbolic meanings for these words often used as symbols in literature.

Glossary of Literary Terms: **http://www.uwm.edu/People/jat/GLOSSARY.HTM**

Dictionary of Literary Terms:
**http://www.bell.k12.ca.us/BellHS/Departments/English/fLiterary.Terms.html.2**

Online Symbolism Dictionary: **http://www.umich.edu/~umfandsf/symbolismproject/symbolism.html**

symbol: _____

ships: _____

flowers: _____

birds: _____

butterflies: _____

serpents: _____

mountains: _____

spiders: _____

eagles: _____

# THE MOCKINGBIRD AS A THEME

Have you ever heard the mockingbird sing? Chances are, once you have heard it, you will never forget its song, although its song may not sound the same from one day to the next. When it sings, it sits high in a tree or on a pole, and its song can be heard in the whole area. The mockingbird, as its name suggests, is a great mimic of not only other birds but has been reported to echo the cackling of a hen and the barking of a dog. It is such a popular and well-loved bird that five states—Arkansas, Texas, Tennessee, Mississippi, and Florida—have all named the mockingbird their state bird. Go to one of these encyclopedia to learn more about this bird with the golden throat.

Grolier Multimedia Encyclopedia Online: **http://gme.grolier.com** (Subscription service)

Encarta Online Home Encyclopedia: **http://encarta.msn.com/EncartaHome.asp**

Walt Whitman wrote about the mockingbird in *Leaves of Grass,* and several Native American tribes told legends about it. One legend told by the Hopis you can read online at the site, "The Rooster, the Mockingbird and the Maiden." The Cherokees, who called it the *huhu,* regarded the mockingbird as almost a supernatural creature, probably because of its ability to imitate other birds.

Out of the Cradle Endlessly Rocking: **http://www.princeton.edu/~batke/logr/log_101.html**

The Rooster, the Mockingbird and the Maiden: **http://www.indians.org/welker/rooster.htm**

The theme of a piece of fiction usually has to do with how people behave. It doesn't preach a message. You must figure out the message of the work of literature yourself. Go to this site and review finding themes.

Analyzing Theme: **http://www.learner.org/exhibits/literature/read/theme1.html**

In *To Kill A Mockingbird,* the mockingbird is a symbol which points to a theme of the story. Two characters in the story are symbolized by the mockingbird, and when Atticus tells Scout and Jem that "it's a sin to kill a mockingbird," the author is also referring to these characters.

**Write two paragraphs.** Write your first paragraph about the mockingbird as a symbol in the story. What did Atticus mean when he said it is a sin to kill a mockingbird? Why is this important in terms of the story? In your second paragraph, write about the mockingbird as a symbol of the two characters in the book and how it relates to the theme of the story. When you're writing your paragraphs, ask yourself these questions?

- Why might Harper Lee have used the mockingbird as a symbol?
- How were the two characters symbolized by the mockingbird? What did they have in common with the bird who does nothing to hurt anyone but sings its heart out to give pleasure?

# AFRICAN-AMERICAN POETRY

Black/white relations are a central part of *To Kill a Mockingbird,* and form the basis for the conflict in the book. Mr. Ewell and many of the characters, including the members of the jury, were prejudiced against black people, and because of their prejudice, they discriminated against them in terrible ways. Some were convicted of crimes for which they were innocent and they were not shown the dignity which Atticus taught the children was a person's by right.

People who discriminate in this way often make the person against whom they are prejudiced feel not as good, or as smart, or as worthy as they feel themselves to be, despite the fact that African Americans have produced many exceptional people who have accomplished great things. One area in which they have excelled is in the writing of poetry. There are many wonderful African American poets.

Using the sites below, name two or more poems by the following poets:

Phat African-American Poetry: **http://members.aol.com/bonvibre/rmp0a.html**

Education First: Black History Activities: **http://www.kn.pacbell.com/wired/bhm/AfroAm.html**

Black-African Related Resources:
**http://www.sas.upenn.edu/African_Studies/Home_Page/mcgee.html**

Langston Hughes: _____

Arna Bontemps: _____

Countee Cullen: _____

Gwendolyn Brooks: _____

Maya Angelou: _____

Rita Dove: _____

Paul Lawrence Dunbar: _____

James Wendell Johnson: _____

Choose one of the poets above, or another African American poet whom you like, and make a book of that poet's work. Place no more than one poem to a page, and write the poems in your best writing or calligraphy. Illustrate your book. **Bonus points:** Include a biography of your poet as part of your book.

# LITERARY TERMS: PUZZLE

The narrator of *To Kill a Mockingbird* is a little girl named Scout Finch. She tells the story. Using the sites below, find the term in literature which matches the definition. Answers go down and across. One two-word answer is T-shaped.

Glossary of Literary Terms: **http://www.uwm.edu/People/jat/GLOSSARY.HTM**

Dictionary of Literary Terms:
**http://www.bell.k12.ca.us/BellHS/Departments/English/fLiterary.Terms.html.2**

1. most important person in story
2. "good character" involved in conflict of story
3. "bad character" involved in story
4. character who is more virtuous than others
5. events which happen one after another in story
6. high point of story when main character "wins"

7. persons or animals in story
8. where and when story takes place
9. wraps up loose ends of the story
10. writes the story
11. minor story events gradually increase
12. tells the story from his/her perspective

**Bonus points:** Name persons or places in *To Kill a Mockingbird* who match numbers 2, 3, 7, 8, 10, and 12.

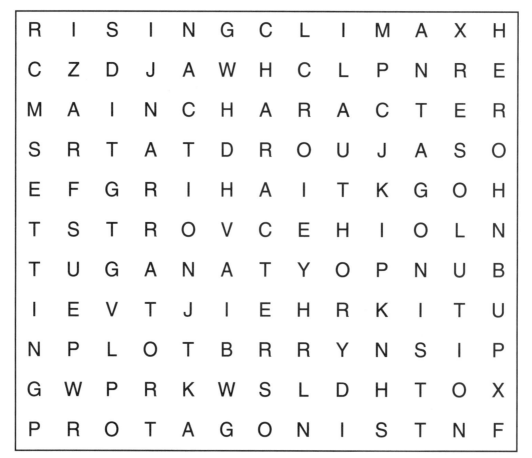

# AN EXAGGERATED STORY

There are many different kinds of stories: love stories, science fiction stories, animal stories, adventure stories, and tall tales, to name a few, but all stories have something in common. A story must have three things. It must have a setting, at least one character, and a plot. Go to these sites and then find and define the following terms:

Dictionary of Literary Terms:
**http://www.bell.k12.ca.us/BellHS/Departments/English/fLiterary.Terms.html.3**

Glossary of Literary Terms: **http://www.uwm.edu/People/jat/GLOSSARY.HTM**

1. Setting _____

2. Character _____

3. Plot _____

A tall tale is a special kind of story in which improbable characters move around and improbable events take place. Tall tales include stories such as those about Paul Bunyan, the bigger-than-life woodsman who strode over mountains and rivers with his huge blue ox, Babe, or the stories of Pecos Bill and Davey Crockett. In other stories, normal people do extraordinary things like sleeping for twenty years, or headless horsemen go riding about the countryside on horseback. Some stories may exaggerate plots or characters without being tall tales.

Mark Twain was an American writer who sometimes wrote stories in which exaggerated events took place, which, if you stretched your imagination a little, you could almost believe really happened. Such a story is Twain's, "The Celebrated Frog of Calaveras County." Go to this site and read this story.

The Celebrated Jumping Frog of Calaveras County:
**http://etext.lib.virginia.edu/railton/huckfinn/jumpfrog.html**

1. What is the setting of this story? _____

2. Name the main character. _____

3. What are three major events in the plot? _____

_____

_____

4. How is this story exaggerated? _____

_____

5. On the back of this page, tell why you believe this story could or could not have really happened.

# NAME THAT AUTHOR!

Did you ever think of a good book you read but were not be able to remember the name of the author? Search engines really come in handy when you want to know a bit of information about a work of literature or an author. Use these, or other ones you know, to find the answers to who wrote each of the following works of literature.

InferenceFind!: **http://infind.inference.com/infind/infind.exe**

Infoseek: **http://www.infoseek.com/**

AltaVista: **http://altavista.digital.com/**

HotBot: **http://wwwhotbot.com/index**

1. *Little Women* _____

2. *The Great Gatsby* _____

3. *A Wrinkle In Time* _____

4. *The Outsiders* _____

5. *I Heard the Owl Call My Name* _____

6. *Cold Mountain* _____

7. *The Joy Luck Club* _____

8. *A Connecticut Yankee in King Arthur's Court* _____

9. *Pygmalion* _____

10. *The Odyssey* _____

11. *The Song of Solomon* _____

12. *The Inferno* _____

13. *The House of Spirits* _____

14. *Jane Eyre* _____

15. *The Handmaid's Tale* _____

16. *Crime and Punishment* _____

17. *Leaves of Grass* _____

# NAME THAT BOOK!

Use a search engine to find two or more books written by each of these authors.

Electric Library: **http://www.elibrary.com/s/geo/**

FINDSPOT: Search Engines + : **http://www.findspot.com/**

Young Adult Reading: **http://www.spruceridge.com/reading/**

Dogpile, the Friendly Multi-Engine Search: **http://www.dogpile.com/**

1. Lawrence Yep _____

2. Henry James _____

3. Charlotte Bronte _____

4. John Steinbeck _____

5. Edith Wharton _____

6. Willa Cather _____

7. Jack London _____

8. Margaret Atwood _____

9. Alice Walker _____

10. Maya Angelou _____

11. John Irving _____

12. Jane Smiley _____

13. Mark Twain _____

14. Charles Dickens _____

15. Ernest Hemingway _____

16. Martin Amis _____

17. Judy Blume _____

18. Cynthia Voight _____

# SHAKESPEARE SCAVENGER HUNT

Using the Internet sites below, find the following information about Shakespeare.

Complete Works of Shakespeare: **http://the-tech.mit.edu/Shakespeare/**

Shakespeare Site Map: **http://daphne.palomar.edu/shakespeare/sitemap.htm**

Shakespeare's Globe: **http://www.reading.ac.uk/globe/Globe.html**

Shakespeare, William: **http://www.encyclopedia.com/articles/11766.html**

Shakespeare Glossary: **http://www.ex.ac.uk/~PEllison/revels/gloss/intro.html**

1. Name of Shakespeare's mother _____

2. Maiden name of Shakespeare's wife _____

3. Names of Shakespeare's three children _____

4. Theater where many of Shakespeare's plays were performed _____

5. River running through London _____

6. Infamous castle in London _____

7. First play written by Shakespeare _____

8. Two Elizabethan weapons _____

9. Date of Shakespeare's birth _____

10. Play in which star-crossed lovers die _____

11. Play in which the Prince of Denmark stars _____

12. A comedy by Shakespeare _____

13. A tragedy by Shakespeare _____

14. A history by Shakespeare _____

15. How are Shakespeare's sonnets titled? _____

**Bonus points:** Complete a time line of Shakespeare's plays or memorize a soliloquy from one of them and present it to the class.

# QUOTATIONS FROM SHAKESPEARE

Quotations from Shakespeare's works fill almost 90 pages in Bartlett's *Familiar Quotations*. Using the quotations sites below, determine the plays from which each of the following quotations come.
**Hint:** Look for the most obvious words of the quotation instead of the whole saying.

Quotations: Reference:

**http://galaxy.tradewave.com/galaxy/Reference/Quotations.html**

Bartlett's Familiar Quotations:

**http://www.columbia.edu/acis/bartleby/bartlett/**

| **Quotation** | **Play** |
| --- | --- |
| 1. To be, or not to be, that is the question. | _____ |
| 2. A horse! A horse! My kingdom for a horse! | _____ |
| 3. What's in a name? | _____ |
| 4. Parting is such sweet sorrow. | _____ |
| 5. Household words | _____ |
| 6. What the dickens | _____ |
| 7. The primrose path | _____ |
| 8. Eaten me out of house and home | _____ |
| 9. Foregone conclusion | _____ |
| 10. Bag and baggage | _____ |
| 11. A lean and hungry look | _____ |
| 12. The game is up. | _____ |

**Bonus points:** Do one or more of the following:

- Use each of the above quotations in a sentence.
- Find the passage in the play from which the quotation comes, and memorize it, and then present it to the class.
- Write a short story in which you use at least six of the quotations.
- Take a survey of people you know to see how many have heard these sayings.

# SOLILOQUIES AND MONOLOGUES FROM SHAKESPEARE

A speech in which a character tells his innermost thoughts to the audience is called a *soliloquy*. Shakespeare's plays contain many soliloquies. Some of the most well-known are these, which you may have heard:

- Hamlet's begins, "To be, or not to be — that is the question."
- Richard III's begins, "Now is the winter of our discontent."
- Romeo's begins, "But, soft! What light through yonder window breaks?"

A speech in which one character speaks at length to others is called a monologue. The difference between a soliloquy and a monologue is that in the first, a character thinks aloud with no one else to hear, while in the second, a character may also be thinking aloud, or not, but others are present to hear what he/she says. Some monologues from Shakespeare's plays include these:

- Polonius's monologue in Hamlet which begins, "To thy own self be true."
- Marc Anthony's in Julius Caesar which begins, "Friends, Romans, countrymen, lend me your ears."
- Mercutio's in Romeo and Juliet which begins, "Oh then, I see Queen Mab hath been with you."

All Shakespeare's plays and poetry were written to be said aloud. The Elizabethans, of whom Shakespeare was one, loved the spoken word. When they went to a play, they went to listen, much as you would listen to a play on the radio, and not just to see it. Learning to read Shakespeare is not as difficult as it might seem with all his unfamiliar words. Here are some hints:

**If possible, watch a film version** of a Shakespearean play. Listen to what is said and how it is said to get a feel for the rhythm of the dialogue. Some lines should be said quickly and others slowly.

**The greatest stress on a line** comes at the end of a sentence. An example of how a Shakespeare line is misunderstood from not stressing the proper words is with the line from Romeo and Juliet, "Wherefore art thou Romeo?" which people sometimes say as though Juliet were asking where he is. If "Romeo" is stressed, as it should be, it is apparent that she is instead asking, "Why are you Romeo, my family's enemy?"

**Pay close attention to punctuation.** When a line ends with a period, stop. If it ends with a comma, pause but do not stop. If the line does not end with punctuation, continue reading without stopping or pausing.

From one of the sites for Shakespeare or quotations, choose a soliloquy or monologue from one of Shakespeare's plays and do the following:

**Practice reading the soliloquy or monologue** and perform it for the class.

**Rewrite the soliloquy in modern English.** Use the Shakespeare glossary to find words you do not understand.

# ROMEO AND JULIET GREETING CARDS

This activity is a good way to learn more about Shakespeare while having fun. There are several sites online where you may send greeting cards to other friends, but not all your friends are online. You will make a greeting card here to send "snail mail" to someone not online, but you will find your greeting online. For your snail mail card, you will need the following:

> paper
>
> lightweight cardboard or construction paper or colorful bits of materials for collage
>
> markers

1. Decide to whom you wish to send a greeting card. It can be a friend, a relative, a teacher, a neighbor—someone you like. A card is always best when it is chosen or written for a certain person. It becomes personal.

2. Use one of the sites below to find lines from Romeo and Juliet which you would like to say to the person who will receive your card.

Complete Works of Shakespeare: **http://the-tech.mit.edu/Shakespeare/works.html**

Mr. Shakespeare Site Map: **http://daphne.palomar.edu/shakespeare/sitemap.htm**

Shakespeare, William: **http://grolier.web.aol.com:8010/post-query/Grolier/Grolier/29585**

Quotations: Reference: **http://galaxy.tradewave.com/galaxy/Reference/Quotations.html**

Bartlett's Familiar Quotations: **http://www.columbia.edu/acis/bartleby/bartlett/**

3. Rewrite the quote in today's language in your best writing or calligraphy.

4. After folding a sheet of paper, lightweight cardboard, or construction paper in half, paste or write your rewritten quote on the inside of your card.

5. Draw, paint, or make a collage of tissue paper and other colorful, soft materials and paste it to the front of your card.

6. Present the card to the person for whom you made it.

# LITERARY FILM FESTIVAL

Many of the great works of literature have been made into movies. Shakespeare's most famous plays have been made into many different movies, as well as operas, musicals, and television programs. *Anne Frank: The Diary of a Young Girl* and *To Kill a Mockingbird* have also been made into movies.

Use the sites below to find the following information on three different movies made from works of literature.

Internet Movie Database Search: **http://us.imdb.com/search.html**

InferenceFind!: **http://www.infind.com/**

Infoseek: **http://www.infoseek.com/**

Choose one which has been made from a play by Shakespeare, such as *Romeo and Juliet, Hamlet, Richard III,* or *Much Ado About Nothing.* Choose two movies made from a novel, a biography, or other story. Some possibilities are *To Kill A Mockingbird, The Diary of Anne Frank, The Outsiders, Sounder,* and *The Miracle Worker.* If you know of another good book made into a movie, choose that.

Name of movie _____

Year made _____

Studio _____

Name of book from which it was made _____

Cast (list of actors playing characters in film) _____

Have you seen this movie? _____

Have you read the book? _____

Comments _____

**Film Festival:** After students have chosen and researched their movies, choose three from all the ones researched by class members and have a film festival. Make posters to advertise the movies. Invite other classes to participate. Show each of the three movies chosen. After the films have been shown, award a "Best of Show" award to the movie and have each student choose one movie about which to write a review. Directions for writing a movie review are on the next page.

# MOVIE REVIEW

**A movie review** is an essay in which the writer discusses a movie he or she has seen and his or her opinion of it. One aspect of a good review is a character analysis of one or more of the characters and how that character is portrayed in the movie. Read some movie reviews available at the sites below. Learn about how to prepare to write a review.

How to Do a Character Analysis: **http://members.aol.com/AACTchAndy/edu/charanaly.html**

Prewriting for Book, Movie or Play Review: **http://leo.stcloud.msus.edu/acadwrite/bookrevpre.html**

Movie Review Query Engine: **http://www.cinema.pgh.pa.us/movie/reviews**

Film Reviews: **http://www.film.com/reviews**

7-9 Book Nook: **http://i-site.on.ca/booknook/79/index.html**

Writing Book Reviews: **http://leo.stcloud.msus.edu/acadwrite/bookrev.html**

Choose one of the movies you saw during your class film festival and write a review on one of them. Use this page to write your preliminary notes for your review and use the sites below to help you write your character analysis and your review essay. You may use the back of this page if you run out of room. When you finish the notes on this page, write your review on your computer word processor and turn it in.

Name of movie _____

Year made _____

Studio _____

Name of book from which it was made _____

Cast of main characters_____

_____

_____

_____

My favorite character in the movie was _____

played by _____ because _____

_____

I would/would not recommend this movie because _____

_____

# BOOKS MADE INTO MOVIES

Many books have been made into movies. A great Internet Site for finding information on movies, including the names of the books from which the movies were made, is this one:

Internet Movie Database Search: **http://us.imdb.com/search.html**

The Internet Movie Database Search will give you the actors and actresses, directors, screenwriters, producers, film company name, and all the nitty-gritty data you want to know about American movies and foreign movies. All you have to do is type in the name of the movie about which you wish information.

Some books which have been made into movies include the following:

> *To Kill a Mockingbird*
> *A Connecticut Yankee in King Arthur's Court*
> *The Adventures of Huckleberry Finn*
> *The Wizard of Oz*
> *Gone with the Wind*
> *Jane Eyre*
> *Pride and Prejudice*
> *The Grapes of Wrath*
> *East of Eden*
> *Little Women*
> *The Good Earth*
> *The Joy Luck Club*
> *All the King's Men*
> *The War of the Worlds*

Plus, most of Shakespeare's plays are in this database.

Other interesting sites with movie information are listed below.

Movie Review Query Engine: **http://www.cinema.pgh.pa.us/movie/reviews**
Film.com: **http://www.film.com**

Academy Awards by Year: **http://us.imdb.com/Oscars/oscars_by_year**
This site is part of the Internet Movie Database and lists all the Oscar winners, including actors, actresses, movies, directors, etc., each year from the first Academy Awards ceremony beginning in 1927-28.

For film reviews, go to this site:
Film Reviews: **http://www.film.com/reviews**

# WRITING PLOT SUMMARIES

**A plot summary** of a piece of fiction consists of three elements: setting, characters, and plot. The summary merely describes the story in its basic form and does not include opinion or evaluation of the story.

Using the Glossary of Literary Terms below, write a definition of each of these terms.

Glossary of Literary Terms: **http://www.uwm.edu/People/jat/GLOSSARY.HTM**

Short Fiction: **http://english-server.hss.cmu.edu/fiction/short.nclk**

Classic Short Stories: **http://www.bnl.com/shorts/**

LEO Process for Writing a Summary: **http://leo.stcloud.msus.edu/acadwrite/summary.html**

Setting _____

Characters _____

Plot _____

Choose a piece of short fiction from one of the sites, read the story, and complete the following notes:

Name of story _____

Author _____

Setting of story _____

Characters in story (Describe the main ones)_____

_____

_____

Main events in plot _____

_____

_____

_____

Using these notes, write a one- to two-page summary (essay) of the story on the word processor of your computer.

# FINDING THEMES

Almost all stories and poems have at least one theme. Some have many. Finding themes in poems or stories is sometimes difficult for students, but it needn't be. To find the theme or themes of a work, you need to decide what the work is about. Ask yourself, what is the main idea of this story or poem? Sometimes a work has more than one theme, so if you find yourself trying to decide between two or more things you think are the theme of the work, it may be because there is more than one theme.

Go to this site and read what a theme is. Then click on *Finding the Theme,* and complete these sentences.

Analyzing Theme: **http://www.learner.org/exhibits/literature/read/theme1.html**

1. The theme of a fable is its _____

2. The theme of a parable is its _____

3. The theme of a piece of fiction is _____

4. List some ways to find the theme in a story. _____

   _____

   _____

   _____

   _____

5. What can a title tell you about a story? _____

6. Review these words at one or both of the following sites:

   symbol _____

   allusion _____

   plot _____

Read a story or poem assigned by your teacher. On the back of this page, tell what you think its theme is. Do you think it has more than one theme? Why? Give examples.

Literary Terms: **http://www.bell.k12.ca.us/BellHS/Departments/English/fLiterary.Terms.html.3**

Online Symbolism Dictionary:
**http://www.umich.edu/%7Eumfandsf/symbolismproject/symbolism.html**

# WRITE AND PUBLISH A BOOK REVIEW

Writing a good book review or book report is more than just retelling its story. When you write a review, you should tell what you did and did not like about the book, and to do this best, you need to ask yourself some questions about the book. Go to this site to learn what kinds of questions you need to ask yourself in order to focus your thinking about the book and enable you to write a good review.

Prewriting a Book Review: **http://leo.stcloud.msus.edu/acadwrite/bookrevpre.html**

1. What are other terms for the what, whom, when, and where questions of a book?

   _____

2. When you evaluate a book, you_____

   _____

Now go to this site:

Writing Book Reviews: **http://leo.stcloud.msus.edu/acadwrite/bookrev.html**

3. What do you include in the introduction to a book review?_____

   _____

4. How should you summarize a nonfiction book?_____

   _____

5. How should you summarize a fiction book?_____

   _____

6. What are the five aspects of your reactions to the book that should you include?_____

   _____

   _____

   _____

   _____

   _____

7. What should you always include with each of these?_____

# BOOK REVIEW CHECKLIST

Use this checklist to plan your next book review and any thereafter. After you complete this checklist, write your review, proofread and rewrite it, and submit it to your teacher and to Book Nook below.

1. _____ Name of book _____

2. _____ Author's name _____

3. _____ Type of book _____

4. _____ Theme(s) of the book_____

5. _____ What is the general problem in the book?_____

_____

Go to this site and review writing a summary.

LEO Process for Writing a Summary: **http://leo.stcould.msus.edu/acadwrite/summary.html**

**Summary**

1. _____ Briefly, this book tells _____

_____

2. _____ Is this book interesting, memorable, entertaining, instructive? Why? _____

_____

3. _____ Do you agree with the author's opinions? Why? _____

_____

4. _____ What issues does the book raise? What does it leave out? _____

_____

5. _____ Relate your opinion of this book as compared to other books or authors._____

_____

6. _____ How did this book affect you? Did it change your opinions? _____

_____

**Submit to:** Book Nook: **http://i-site.on.ca/booknook.html**

52

# CITING SOURCES

When you write any kind of essay, book report, or research paper, you must cite your sources. What this means is that you must give credit to the author of a work from which you take information, or to whomever you quote in your own writing. It is illegal to copy the writing of someone else and claim it as your own. Go to the dictionary and find the definition of plagiarism.

WWWebster Dictionary: **http://www.m-w.com/dictionary**

**plagiarism:** _____

This is one of the most important things you must know about writing. Almost all writing, except that which is old enough to have become what is called public domain, is covered under international copyright laws. These laws must not be violated.

MLA Citations: **http://www.hcc.hawaii.edu/education/hcc/library/mlahcc.html**

Walker Style Sheet: **http://www.cas.usf.edu/english/walker/mla.html**

There are generally acceptable ways to cite information. Go to these sites. What information will you include for each of these sources?

electronic (Internet) sources: _____

_____

encyclopedias and reference books: _____

_____

books: _____

_____

magazines: _____

_____

newspaper articles: _____

_____

more than one author: _____

_____

more than one source by the same author: _____

_____

# PARTS OF SPEECH POETRY

It's difficult to define exactly what a poem is, because there are so many different kinds of poems. Poems take many shapes and forms, but always have structure imposed upon them by the poet and are written in lines which may or may not be sentences. The poem you are going to write here is not written in sentences, although the fourth line may be.

You are going to write a poem called the diamante, because it is shaped like a diamond. Go to the Poetry Pals site to see what a diamante poem looks like. Look at one closely and you'll see that it is written according to certain rules:

**Line one:** a noun, which is also the subject.

**Line two:** two adjectives which describe the subject.

**Line three:** three -ing words which show the subject as he/she generally is or tell how the subject behaves.

**Line four:** four words about the subject. This line can be a statement, or a sentence, about the subject. It should consist of four words which describe, tell about, or show the person being himself/herself in some way which is significant to you, the poet. It may be a sentence which shows the subject changing in some way, or showing another aspect of that subject.

**Line five:** three -ing words—these should be different from the ones in line three and should reflect what has been said in line four.

**Line six:** two adjectives which describe the subject—again, these should reflect the subject as he/she/it appears in line four.

**Line seven:** a noun which is a synonym for the subject and which reflects what has been said in the previous three lines

When your poem is finished, it should be shaped like a diamond, and you may need to move words around a little to accomplish this.

Poetry Pals Forms and Samples:
**http://www.geocities.com/EnchantedForest/5165/poetry_samples.html**

What is a Noun? **http://www.uottawa.ca/academic/arts/writcent/hypergrammar/nouns.html**

What is an adjective? **http://www.uottawa.ca/academic/arts/writcent/hypergrammar/adjective.html**

Synonym Dictionary: **http://vancouver-webpages.com/synonyms.html**

# ADJECTIVE SYNONYMS

Finish this sentence by referring to the following sites. Then, find synonyms for the listed words and use the synonyms in sentences.

An adjective _____

WWWebster Thesaurus: **http://www.m-w.com/thesaurus.htm**

Roget's Internet Thesaurus: **http://www.thesaurus.com/thesaurus/**

Synonym Dictionary: **http://vancouver-webpages.com/synonyms.html**

What is an Adjective?: **http://www.uottawa.ca/academic/arts/writcent/hypergrammar/adjectve.html**

mischievous _____

negligible _____

paradoxical _____

scruffy _____

ingenuous _____

homogeneous _____

robust _____

tantalizing _____

unorthodox _____

gargantuan _____

bellicose _____

constructive _____

dogmatic _____

gullible _____

meticulous _____

prior _____

shrewd _____

# PREPOSITIONAL PHRASES

Using the following sites for information, complete these sentences.

What is a preposition?:
**http://www.uottawa.ca/academic/arts/writcent/hypergrammar/preposit.html**

Owl Handouts in Outline Form: **http://owl.english.purdue.edu/writers/by-topic.html**

Guide to Grammar and Writing: **http://webster.commnet.edu/HP/pages/darling/grammar.htm**

A preposition links _____

A preposition answers the questions _____

or _____ .

List twenty or more prepositions on the back of this page.

A preposition introduces_____

A prepositional phrase is made up of _____

**Underline the prepositional phrases in these sentences.**

We had been to the theater once and went again for our anniversary.

Please hand me the cake on the table, and I will cut a slice for each of you.

In the middle of the night, we heard an explosion and jumped out of bed.

You will find that book in the library in the reference section.

By the stairway is a stand where you may hang your coat.

When you drive by the ocean this time of year, you may see whales.

It's important for you to fill out this paper before school begins in the fall.

Joshua jumped into the swimming pool wearing all his clothes.

Shirley will go with us to the mall because she wants to get out of the house.

On the calendar I have marked all the family birthdays so I won't forget them.

In "South Pacific" Mary Martin sang, "I am as corny as Kansas in August."

# GRAMMAR TREASURE HUNT

The Internet contains several excellent sites for writing and grammar, including the ones below. Use at least two of these sites to complete the following exercise. For each, cite the section of the site where you found your answer. You may use the back of the page to complete your answers.

Guide to Grammar and Writing: **http://webster.commnet.edu/HP/pages/darling/grammar.htm**

Owl Handouts: **http://owlenglish.purdue.edu/writers/by-topic.html**

HyperGrammar: **http://www.uottawa.ca/academic/arts/writcent/hypergrammar/**

Online English Grammar: **http://www.edunet.com/english/grammar/**

**Name the eight parts of speech.**_____

_____

**What is a sentence fragment?** _____

_____

**What is an independent clause?** _____

_____

**Write a run-on sentence.** _____

_____

**What is wrong with this sentence?  The boys is going to town together.** _____

_____

**How are most plurals formed?** _____

_____

**What are pronouns and pronoun antecedents?**_____

_____

**What do verb tenses show?** _____

_____

# GRAMMAR TREASURE HUNT (cont.)

**What is a dependent clause?** _____

_____

**How is a phrase different from a clause?** _____

_____

**Write one sentence in the active voice.** _____

_____

**Write one sentence in the passive voice.** _____

_____

**Which of the above two sentences is better and why?** _____

_____

**Give an example of a prepositional phrase.** _____

_____

**What two things does every complete sentence contain?** _____

_____

**Make each of these nouns possessive: girl, children, woman, fox, goat.** _____

_____

**How can you tell if a verb has a direct object?** _____

_____

**What is a linking verb?** _____

_____

**What is a complement?** _____

_____

# DIAGRAMMING SENTENCES

Sometimes diagramming a sentence helps us to understand how the words in a sentence go together.

Begin with a base line. Place the subject on the left side of the line, the predicate verb on the right side. If there is a direct object, place it to the right of the verb with a straight up-and-down line separating them.

subject | verb | object      John | reads | comic books

If there is a predicate adjective or a predicate noun, place it to the right of the verb with a slanted line separating them.

subject | verb / predicate adj. or predicate noun

Mrs. Hopkins | is / my teacher

Place adjectives and adverbs on slanted lines under the words they modify. Example: My older sister goes to New York every year.

sister | goes
\ my          \ to          \ year
  \ older          \ New York          \ every

Place prepositional phrases, like "to New York," on slanted and horizontal lines under the words they modify. "To New York" modifies "goes" by telling *where* my older sister goes. "Every year" modifies "goes" by telling *when* she goes. An indirect object would go under the verb like this prepositional phrase, but with the (to) in parentheses.

If you are unsure which word an adjective or adverb modifies, ask yourself to what does it refer? For example, in the sentence above, "my" and "older" describe sister. Use the sections on sentence construction in these sites to help you decide how to diagram each of the sentences on the following page.

Guide to Grammar and Writing: **http://webster.commnet.edu/HP/pages/darling/grammar.htm**

HyperGrammar: **http://www.uottawa.ca/academic/arts/writcent/hypergrammar/**

Review Parts of the Sentence:
**http://www.uottawa.ca/academic/arts/writcent/hypergrammar/rvsentpt.html**

# DIAGRAMMING SENTENCES *(cont.)*

1. The stories in this book are very exciting.

2. Cicily isn't going to the dance at school.

3. One has to order tickets early for some Broadway musicals.

4. Jack heard on the radio an announcement about the movie.

5. I have lived at 14 Niagara Way since 1993.

6. The Valley of the Moon is the heart of California's wine region.

7. John wrote his essay in two hours.

# JABBERWOCKY GRAMMAR

Do you think you don't understand grammar? Do you have trouble remembering what an adjective is or when to use this pronoun or that one? Don't feel like the Lone Ranger if you do. Many people feel the same way. But you may know more than you think you know about English.

If you are a native speaker of English, you have a built-in English grammar you learned as you learned to speak. You know without having to think about it where to place nouns, verbs, and the other parts of speech in your daily speaking, but sometimes it helps to practice how to label them.

You can recognize nouns and verbs even when you do not know what they mean. In fact, you can recognize them by their context, the way in which they are used, even when they are not real words but are nonsense words.

**Review nouns and verbs** at the sites What is a Noun? and Guide to Grammar and Writing.

What is a Noun?: **http://www.uottawa.ca/academic/arts/writcent/hypergrammar/nouns.html**

Guide to Grammar and Writing: **http://webster.commnet.edu/HP/pages/darling/grammar.htm**

**Find the poem "Jabberwocky"** and print it from the site below.

*Through the Looking Glass,* Chapter 1:
**http://www.literature.org/Works/Lewis-Carroll/through-the-looking-glass/chapter-01.html**

**Read the poem line by line.** Draw one line under the nouns and two lines under the verbs. Do you recognize any words? What words do you recognize? How can you identify most of the nouns?

**Rewrite the poem in standard English** revealing what you think is its real meaning.

**Compare your work** with that of your classmates'. How many different ideas did you come up with? This is because you know from a lifetime of speaking English how to recognize nouns and verbs and you have been given little clue as to what their meanings are. Does it help if you read the poem with the rest of the chapter?

**Complete the same exercise with "What the White Rabbit Said,"** from *Alice In Wonderland,* Chapter 12. How is this poem different from "Jabberwocky"? Do you understand it better than you did "Jabberwocky"?

*Alice's Adventures in Wonderland,* Chapter 12:
**http://www.literature.org/Works/Lewis-Carroll/alice-in-wonderland/chapter-12.html**

# WRITING SENTENCES

The basic part of most writing is the sentence. Go to this site and fill in the blanks.

Subject and Predicate:
**http://www.uottawa.ca/academic/arts/writcent/hypergrammar/subjpred.html**

1. A sentence contains _____ and _____

2. To find the subject of a sentence, _____

3. An imperative sentence gives _____

4. The word "there" is the subject _____

5. A subject is built around a _____ or a _____

6. A predicate is built around one or more _____

    Go to this site and fill in the blanks:

    Guide to Grammar and Writing: **http://webster.commnet.edu/HP/pages/darling/grammar.htm**

7. A sentence fragment cannot _____

8. A run-on sentence _____

    Go to this site and fill in the blanks:

    Useful Definitions of Sentences: **http://owl.english.purdue.edu/Files/1.html**

9. An independent clause is _____

10. A dependent clause is _____

11. Can an independent clause be a sentence? _____
    Why? _____

12. Can a dependent clause be a sentence? _____
    Why? _____

13. Write a complete sentence here. _____

Also check out Sentence Craft: **http://humanitas.ucsb.edu/users/behrens/cid/tc.htm**

# IDENTIFYING SENTENCES

Using this site, identify the following as a simple sentence (SS), compound sentence (CP), complex sentence (CX), independent clause (Ind), dependent clause (Dep), fused sentence (FS), or run-on sentence (R-O). Some items may be two different things.

Building Sentence Patterns: **http://leo.stcloud.msus.edu/punct/sentpatt.html**

1. _____ Because he wanted to do something else.
2. _____ Joni got up and got dressed then she made her bed.
3. _____ We love to go to the movies don't you?
4. _____ If I wash the sheets, will you make the bed?
5. _____ Sometimes it just doesn't pay to get up in the morning.
6. _____ Mr. Morgan gave his horse a carrot, and then he brushed him down.
7. _____ I think learning to write correctly is fun.
8. _____ When the dogs began to bark and jump around the yard.
9. _____ It's easy to write a simple sentence, but sometimes it's harder to think of a good one to write.
10. _____ When we went to Paris, we saw the Eiffel Tower.

**Rewrite this sentence correctly at least three different ways.**

Johnny won the marathon he hadn't been in training long.

_____

_____

_____

Complete the review exercises for subject and predicate at this site.

Subject and Predicate:
**http://www.uottawa.ca/academic/arts/writcent/hypergrammar/subjpred.html**

Go to this site and add your contribution to what is probably the world's longest run-on sentence. What will you do to make sure it remains a run-on?

The Amazing run-On Sentence Page: **http://members.aol.com/laninaia01/runon.html**

# VARYING YOUR SENTENCES

Read this paragraph:

> John wanted a package of bubble gum. He went to the store. The clerk said he didn't have any bubble gum. John went to another store. He bought some bubble gum there.

That may be one of the most boring paragraphs you have ever read—just a series of short, choppy sentences strung together. While you're not likely to make anything exciting out of this, you can vary the sentences and combine them into one or two longer sentences which will prevent their being quite so deadly. Go to Sentence Craft and study the many different ways in which you may vary the length and style of your sentences by combining them into compound and complex ones. Click on the links which give answers to the following.

Sentence Craft: **http://humanitas.ucsb.edu/users/behrens/cid/tc.htm**

1. What is a compound sentence? _____

   _____

2. Name at least three ways you can compound a sentence._____

   _____

   _____

3. What does a direct object do? _____

   _____

4. Write a sentence with a direct object. _____

_____

You can vary your sentences by combining clauses, changing short sentences into prepositional phrases, combining subjects, combining predicates, and many other ways. How many different ways can you think of to vary your sentences? Practice a few on the back of this page.

Study the examples in Sentence Craft and Sentence Builder below, and then go to the next page and practice combining short sentences into longer ones which are more varied and interesting to read. You may refer to these sites, if you need to do so.

Sentence Builder: **http://www2.actden.com/writ_den/tips/sentence/**

# PRACTICE COMBINING SENTENCES

Combine each of these sets of short sentences into one longer, compound sentence.

1. The high school is going to have a dance.
   Jeremy asked Brittany to go to the dance.
   Brittany had another date already.
   Jeremy was disappointed.
   Jeremy doesn't know if he will go to the dance now.

2. Aardvark Airlines is having a special.
   The special is on air fares.
   It is to get more people to fly with Aardvark.
   Some fares are more than half off.
   I might go to visit my friends in New York.

3. The storm caused damage.
   The damage was to several houses.
   The houses are on my street.
   There was a lot of damage.
   Some roofs lost shingles.

4. The main library is just opening its new building.
   They have been working on it for two years.
   It has a big dome.
   It has a tiled roof.
   The ribbon-cutting ceremony will be Friday.

5. My brother plays football.
   He is the center on the high school varsity team.
   He plays first string.
   I don't like football because it's too rough.
   He gets mad because I won't go to the games.

6. Spring has sprung.
   Flowers are blooming all around the neighborhood.
   There are red, pink, yellow, white, and blue flowers.
   Some people don't like it when all the flowers bloom.
   They sneeze, their eyes water, and their noses run.
   I'm glad I don't have allergies.

**Go to the exercise on Sentence Combining and try your luck at combining the short sentences there into longer ones. Be careful not to make run-on sentences out of them. When you finish this exercise, add to the world's largest run-on sentence at this site.**

The Run-On Sentence page: **http://members.aol.com/laninaia01/runon.html**

# WRITING PARAGRAPHS

When writing a paragraph for school papers, reports, and essays you need to follow a regular format. Just as the basic format for writing a five-paragraph essay consists of writing an introductory paragraph, a body of supporting details, and a conclusion, a good paragraph consists of an introduction, supporting details and a concluding, or closing, sentence. Go to this site and use it to help you fill in the blanks below.

Paragraph Builder: **http://www2.actden.com/writ_den/tips/paragrap/**

1. The introductory sentence of a paragraph is the _____

2. What does it state?_____

3. The _____ give details about the opening sentence.

4. They include _____, _____, and _____

5. The closing sentence of a paragraph restates _____

6. Define the prewriting stage of writing a paragraph. _____

   _____

7. The writing state is when_____

8. When editing paragraphs, do the following:

   a. _____

   b. _____

   c. _____

   d. _____

   e. _____

   f. _____

   g. _____

List eight kinds of paragraphs:

# WRITE E-MAIL TO A PEN PAL

E-mail is rapidly becoming the universal communication tool. Most people's first online experience begins with hooking up the modem to the computer and telephone, then sending and receiving e-mail. E-mail is an excellent way for teachers to introduce their students to students in other schools, cities, states and countries. Fortunately, there are resources for teachers who want to provide this opportunity to their students in a safe, educational environment.

Some of the activities students may engage in with e-mail:

- Exchange poetry and creative writing with students around the world.

- Establish "sister" schools with schools around the world.

- Learn about other cultures by direct exchange of ideas.

- Share projects and writing.

- Exchange greeting cards and holiday wishes with students around the world.

- Establish friendships with students around the world.

Parents may be uneasy about allowing students to write to strangers in an uncontrolled situation, but there are available to teachers services which allow the exchange of e-mail and ideas safely, including the following:

Intercultural E-Mail Classroom Connections: **http://www.stolaf.edu/network/iecc/**

Intercultural E-Mail Classroom Connections is a free service offered by St. Olaf College to help teachers and classes link with partners in other countries and cultures for e-mail pen pal and classroom project exchanges. Classrooms in approximately seventy countries participate in this program.

Classroom Webs: **http://www.classroom.net/classweb/**

With Classroom Webs you can connect with other schools. Maybe you'd like to find another school with the same name as yours, or maybe you would like to connect with a school in a particular city in another part of the country or the world. This is the place to go to find the Web site address of that school. The state, province, and country searches are not as accurate as the ones for schools and cities, however.

E-Mail Key pal Connection: **http://www.comenius.com/keypal/**

E-Mail Key pal Connection is an international e-mail connection service. This one is not free and costs a lifetime registration fee of $14.95 which provides three pen pals for the fee.

For detailed information on writing, sending, and receiving e-mail, see *Internet for Teachers and Parents*.

# PUNCTUATION—QUOTATION MARKS

Dialogue can make or break a story which is otherwise good. Dialogue, what the characters say, fulfills several functions in a story.

- Dialogue reveals the personalities of the characters in two ways:
    - By showing what a character thinks of himself.
    - By showing what other characters think of him.
- Dialogue also reveals the relationships of the characters to each other and the conflict of the story—what makes the plot move ahead.

Go to these sites to learn how to punctuate dialogue. Read, especially, about the different places commas and periods go in different sentences, depending on where the explanatory words (the he said; she said) are placed. Then punctuate the following sentences:

Purdue Owl Handouts—Quotation Marks: **http://owl.english.purdue.edu/Files/l4.html**

Guide to Grammar and Writing: **http://webster.commnet.edu/HP/pages/darling/grammar.htm**

1. Jake said I don't want to go to the movie. I want to go to the ball game

2. We can't go to the ball game or the movie today said Dad We have too many things to do at home today

3. I have to plan for my birthday party next week said Lindsay and I need to ask Mom what I can have to eat We need to go shopping

4. Dad looked a little flustered Right now he said we need to get the house cleaned Your mother will be home soon and we told her we'd take care of things for her

5. I hate to clean house Jake said I'd rather play outside with my friends

6. You're always complaining I'll be glad when you're older Little brothers can be such pests Lindsay said

7. Jake when your room is clean and all your things are picked up around here you can go outside to play said Dad Right now we have work to do Play can wait

8. Hello Is everybody home Mother's voice sounded from the front door

9. Mom Jake's being such a pest and I need to plan my party and all Dad says is we have to clean house said Lindsay

10. We sure don't sound like the Cleaver family Dad grinned at Mom

# WRITE A STORY USING SPECIFIC ACTION VERBS

The two most important kinds of words in English are nouns and verbs. Nouns are the who's and the what's about which you write. Verbs are the words which carry all the action of a story. Any story must be written for a reader, whether that reader is your teacher, a friend, or someone you don't even know. When that reader reads what you have written, he/she wants to "see" what is happening. You must "show" that reader.

You can show your reader what you want him/her to see by using specific action verbs. The word "walk" just won't do when you want your reader to see your character walking in a certain way. Even adding adverbs to the verb will not give your reader a picture. In fact, adverbs used too frequently can be deadly for your story. Use this thesaurus or the one from Webster's Dictionary to find specific verbs to use instead of the verbs and adverbs given. Find as many of each as you can.

Roget's Internet Thesaurus: **http://www.thesaurus.com/thesaurus/**

WWWebster Dictionary: **http://www.m-w.com/dictionary**

walk slowly _____

walk quickly _____

speak loudly _____

speak softly _____

cry pitifully _____

laugh brayingly _____

jump crazily _____

move forward _____

move backward _____

want badly _____

Go to the next page for story starters to use to begin your story.

# STORY STARTERS

Choose one of these story starters as the beginning of your story. Each story starter has a setting, two characters, and two events in the story. Add other events and characters to the story as you wish. Use specific active verbs in your story. You may not use any of these taboo words unless they are spoken by a character in the story.

Taboo words: walk, talk, speak, cry, laugh, cute, pretty, good, bad, happy, sad, fun

|  |  |
|---|---|
| **Setting:** | a shopping mall on a Saturday afternoon |
| **Characters:** | Jan and Marisa, both fourteen years old |
| **Events:** | Someone takes a radio from a store without paying for it |
|  | Marisa buys a new pair of jeans. |
| **Setting:** | the beach during summer vacation |
| **Characters:** | Justin, aged fifteen, and Jeremy, aged fourteen |
| **Events:** | Someone kicks sand in Jeremy's face. |
|  | The lifeguard swims out to rescue a swimmer who calls for help. |
| **Setting:** | the arcade in the movie theater on a Friday night |
| **Characters:** | Jeff, aged thirteen, and Carter, aged sixteen |
| **Events:** | Someone wins a game. |
|  | Someone is accused of cheating. |
| **Setting:** | the football field during Field Day |
| **Characters:** | Leslie, a cheerleader, and Tanner, a spectator |
| **Events:** | A player breaks a leg. |
|  | An unknown person appears on the field. |
| **Setting:** | in the attic of Chelsea's house on a rainy winter day |
| **Characters:** | Chelsea and her friend Kendall |
| **Events:** | Chelsea and Kendall open a big, old chest they find in the attic. |
|  | A magical kingdom appears. |

**Write your story. Include dialogue in your story.**

**Proofread it for spelling and punctuation errors. Double-check to make sure you did not use any of the taboo words above.**

**Double-check to make sure you used only active verbs.**

**Submit your story for publication online.**

Active/Passive Verbs: **http://owl.english.purdue.edu/Files/112.html**

Creative Writing Opportunities: **http://kidswriting.miningco.com/library/weekly/aa050897.htm**

KidPub: **http://www.kidpub.org/kidpub/howto.html**

# WRITING A SHORT MYSTERY STORY

Mystery stories are a favorite kind of story for people of all ages, and they range from children's mystery books like the ones about Nancy Drew and the Hardy Boys to adult mysteries by Agatha Christie and all the many wonderful mystery writers in the field of popular fiction.

What is a mystery story? It's a story in which some sort of puzzle, unknown, or secret causes a problem for a character or characters, who want to discover the answer to the problem, or solve it. Why do people read mystery stories? They read them for the same reasons people read other kinds of literature. Go to this site and learn the many reasons given there for the reading of literature.

What Makes a Good Short Story?: **http://www.learner.org/exhibits/literature/**

Name four reasons people read literature.

1. _____

2. _____

3. _____

4. _____

You are going to read, "A Jury of Her Peers," a short mystery story by Susan Glaspell. Before you do, review the following terms at the sites below so that you can identify them in the story. These terms are the **elements** of a story.

The **setting** of a story is _____

The **characters** of a story are_____

The **plot** of a story is _____

**Point of view** is _____

Constructing Plot: **http://www.learner.org/exhibits/literature/read/plot1.html**

Creating Character: **http://www.learner.org/exhibits/literature/read/charact1.html**

Describing Setting: **http://www.learner.org/exhibits/literature/read/setting1.html**

Point of View: **http://www.learner.org/exhibits/literature/read/pov1.html**

**Return to the first site and enter the door to the story, "A Jury of Her Peers." Print the story to read it or read it online. As you read, complete the following page by identifying all the elements of this story.**

# WRITING A SHORT MYSTERY STORY *(cont.)*

Name of story _____

Author _____

Setting _____

Characters _____

Point of view _____

**Identify the plot by supplying the following information:** You may use the back of the page to complete your answers.

In the beginning of the story _____ wanted _____,

but _____

and then _____

and _____

Finally _____

This is the simplest way to identify plot, of course. The plot of a good story has many more details than you have been asked to supply here, but this will give you an idea of how a very basic plot is created.

## Write a Mystery Story!

Now you're ready to write a mystery story of your own, but before you do the actual writing, you need to lay some groundwork. Just as a foundation must be laid for a house before the walls and roof go up, the foundation of a story must be laid before the actual sentences and paragraphs are written. While you do this, you may refer to the material you read on the elements of a story.

You also may want to review how to punctuate dialogue, because if your story is to read like something that really happened, you will probably want to include dialogue in it. Review page 68, or you may refer to these sites:

Purdue Owl Handouts Quotation Marks: **http://owl.english.purdue.edu/Files/14.html**

Guide to Grammar and Writing: **http://webster.commnet.edu/HP/pages/darling/grammar.htm**

At the second site, click on "Punctuation Marks Besides the Comma," and when you get to the chart of punctuation marks, click on the quotation marks. ("")

# WRITING A SHORT MYSTERY STORY *(cont.)*

First, determine what your setting will be. This is a very important part of the story. If the setting of a story is changed, the entire story will be different.

**Where the story will take place** _____

**When the story will take place** _____

Next create your **characters.** It sometimes helps to make a **character chart.** Put the names of your main characters at the tops of the columns, and then fill in information for each of them.

Name _____     _____

Hair color _____     _____

Eye color _____     _____

Age _____     _____

Grade _____     _____

Hobbies _____     _____

Family _____     _____

And because you want to give your characters personalities, list a couple of the favorite sayings of each.

_____     _____

_____     _____

You want to give your main character(s) a problem to solve, because this is what will lead to the events which occur in the plot.

My character's problem is _____

_____

Now, at long last, you're ready to write your story. Write it once just as it comes to you. Then go back, read what you have written, and make changes as you need to do so. Does your story make sense? If not, why? What can you do to change it so it does make sense? Rewrite your story with the corrections you have made.

Advice for Young Writers: **http://www.inkspot.com/young/articles/advice.html**

Go to this site for "Advice for Young Writers," a series of articles by the writers of fiction for young people with personal advice on how to become a good writer.

# WHAT IS FICTION?

**Fiction** is the imaginative telling of stories. There are different kinds of fiction, some of which have come down to us from days past by word of mouth and some which have come to us through the printed word. Stories which have come to us by word of mouth include fables, myths, folklore, and legends. Stories which have come to us by the printed page include short stories and novels. There is overlap among them, of course. Some myths, legends, and folklore were also written down; however, they were originally told orally.

To begin this unit on fiction, you need to know how to tell the difference between one kind of fiction called a genre, and the others. Use your online dictionary or thesaurus to find the definitions of these genres of fiction and give an example of each.

WWWebster Dictionary: **http://www.m-w.com/dictionary**

Roget's Internet Thesaurus: **http://www.thesaurus.com/thesaurus/**

Oxford English Dictionary: **http://www.oed.com**

Book Nook 7-9: **http://i-site.on.ca/booknook/79/index.html**

**fable** _____

    example _____

**folklore** _____

    example _____

**myth** _____

    example _____

**legend** _____

    example _____

**short story** _____

    example _____

**novel** _____

    example _____

# READ AND WRITE FABLES

The **fable** has been one of the favorite kinds of stories of all time. Fables have been told for thousands of years. The best known fables are probably those first recorded by Aesop, but there have been fables told in almost every society in the world, including the Native Americans of North America.

The two characteristics of a fable:

- Fables contain personification.
- Fables teach a moral.

**Find the definitions of these words in your online dictionary (p. 16).**

personification_____

moral _____

**From one of the collections below, choose a fable by Aesop and answer these questions.**

How is there personification in this fable?_____

_____

What is the moral of this fable? _____

_____

**Choose one of the Native American fables from the collection of Myths and Legends of the Sioux below and answer these questions.**

How is there personification in this fable?_____

_____

What is the moral of this fable? _____

_____

**Write a fable of your own which includes personification and a moral.** At the site Animals, Myths & Legends, send your story to Oban.

Aesop's Fables: **gopher://spinaltap.micro.umn.edu/11/Ebooks/By%20Title/aesop**

Aesop's Fables: Online Collection: **http://www.pacficnet.net/~johnr/aesop**

Native American Legends: **http://www.spindle.net/lotto/native26.html**

Animals, Myths & Legends: **http://www.ozemail.com.au/~oban/index.html**

# MYTHS AND LEGENDS

Myths and legends have come down to us from so long ago that no one knows how long they've been around. These are the stories which have answered questions people have always had, questions like these:

**How did the world begin?**

**How did people come to be?**

**When did the sun first come into the world?**

**Did animals once act like people?**

**How did good and evil come into the world?**

Sometimes we think mythology was important just to the Greeks and Romans. But all peoples of the world have had myths and legends, not just the Greeks and Romans. These stories are about the people and where they came from, what they believe, and why they do as they do.

Many of these stories contain the wisdom of the people who told them. They told people what happens when certain rules of society are not obeyed, why they are as they are, why some things are important and others not so important. They give us insight into how people have lived with nature, and what their relationships with each other and with animals have been. They tell who their heroes were and why they were heroes.

Myths and legends tell a people who they are and why they and their way of life is important to them. It's been said that people need stories as much as they need food and water. Maybe that is because myths and legends tell a people there was beginning to everything, and there is a reason things go on as they do. They put order into what would otherwise be chaos.

Choose one of the sites below. Each of these sites has many different myths and legends to choose from. This is an opportunity for you to explore a part of our literary heritage which is rich and colorful, as well as meaningful. Be prepared to exercise your mouse finger as you travel through the land of mythology online.

Folklore, Myth, and Legend: **http://pubpages.unh.edu/~cbsiren/myth.html**

General Folklore and Mythology: **http://pibweb.it.nwu.edu/~pib/mythgene.htm**

Folklore and Mythology Electronic Texts: **http://www.pitt.edu/%7Edash/folktexts.html**

7-9 Book Nook: **http://i-site.on.ca/booknook/79/index.html**

# MYTHS AND LEGENDS WORKSHEET

**Find from any two cultures myths about how the world began.** These stories are often called creation myths. Label your stories Myth A and Myth B. As you read the stories, compare them using the Venn diagram on the next page. Tell how Myth A is different from Myth B in the space to the left and how Myth B is different from Myth A in the space to the right. In the center, list ways in which the two myths are similar. Ask these questions, and others you think of, about the stories as you complete the diagram.

**Who or what created the world, or did it just happen?**

**What was created first? second? third?**

**Is any reason given for why the world was created?**

**Who were the first people?**

**How did they come to be?**

**Is there any reason given for why people were created?**

**Were the people told how they should live? If so, how?**

**Were the sun, moon, and stars created at the same time as the earth?**

**How and why were the sun, moon, and stars created?**

**Find myths from two cultures about their gods and/or goddesses.** Using the Venn diagram, compare the gods and/or goddesses in the same way you did the creation story above. Ask these questions, and others you think of, about the stories you read.

**How many gods and/or goddesses did they believe in?**

**What were their gods like?**

**Did they have many gods or one?**

**What relationship did the people have with their gods? Were they afraid of them? Friends with them? Did they joke about them, or were they serious about them?**

**Write a compare/contrast essay.** In your essay, use your Venn diagrams to illustrate how the stories you read were alike and how they were different. What conclusions can you draw from what you learned about the stories?

**Bonus points: Find a story about a catastrophe,** such as one which destroyed the world at some time. For example, many cultures have stories about a great flood which destroyed what the people knew as the world. Use your word processor to write the story (retell it) in your own words.

# MYTHOLOGY VENN DIAGRAM

Myth B

Myth A

# LET'S HEAR IT FOR THE LITTLE PEOPLE!

Folklore often includes the antics of Little People who play tricks on others. The Cherokee told stories of how Little People would move things you needed when you weren't looking, then sit back in the shadows and giggle while you tried to find them. Lttle People loved to play jokes on the unsuspecting.

The Micmac of the Northeast told stories about Little People who stayed indoors during the day and came out only at night when they loved to dance and have parties. At night, they sang and danced, played the drums, and had a jolly good time. Usually they were helpful, but sometimes they were full of mischief, and they had magical powers! They could shrink you down to their size as long as you were with them, but when you left them, you returned to your original size.

Some of the most famous Little People are the leprechauns of Ireland, little green shoemakers who guard pots of gold which they will allow you to take from them, but only if you can catch them and hold onto them first. Sometimes these little folk fall in love with humans. In Finian's Rainbow, a musical theater show, Og, a leprechaun, falls in love with Susan, a human. Og is fickle however; he sings about how he loves Susan, but when he's near another girl, he loves her, too.

English and Irish folklores are full of Little People, usually called fairies (faeries). In Shakespeare's *Midsummer Night's Dream,* a whole fairy kingdom mimicked the Elizabethan society of nobility all the way down to ordinary beings and workers. In one production of the play, two fairies, Titania and Puck, swung on trapezes while the humans, who could not see them, went on about their silly ways. Most Elizabethans believed in fairies and thought that anywhere you walked in the woods, they would be there to observe you as you went about your business.

Mary Norton's novel *The Borrowers,* made into a movie in 1997 and a favorite of children everywhere, is about a family of people who are only four inches high and live under the floorboards of a house in England. They furnish their miniature home with bits and scraps left lying around by the full-sized humans in the house.

At the sites below, learn more about leprechauns and fairies, and then complete the activity on the next page.

Leprechauns: **http://www.bconnex.net/%7Embuchana/realms/stpatric/leprecan.html**

Irish Fairy and Folktales by William Butler Yeats:
**http://faeryland.tamu-commerce.edu/~earendil/faerie/Yeats/index.html**

The Irish Fairy Folk: **http://www.ncf.carleton.ca/~bj333/faries.html**

# CREATE A LITTLE PERSON

Create a Little Person of your own. This is to be a very special little person, and you can let your imagination fly. The first thing you need to do is create a history for this tiny being.

Use the questions below to plan, and then make a small scene in a box (a diorama), showing your little person going about his/her normal duties.

Make a small poster describing your little person and place it in front of your diorama.

Write a story of how you first learned about your little person.

Name _____

Where does this little person come from? _____

Have you ever seen this little person? _____

If you've never seen this little person, how do you know he/she exists?_____

_____

Describe your little person:

      Hair color _____

      Eye color _____

      Size _____

What sort of clothing does your little person wear? _____

_____

What does your little person do during the day? _____

_____

What does your little person do during the night?_____

_____

Is your little person mischievous? How?_____

_____

# PRINCES AND PRINCESSES, WITCHES AND FROGS

Fairy tales have been around for hundreds, maybe even thousands, of years. Not all stories called fairy tales are about fairies, of course, and there's no way of knowing how they came to be called that, but all stories called fairy tales have certain things in common.

**Fairy tales are stories about princes and princesses, witches, elves, hobgobblins, and magical events.** In them, impossible things become possible, and fantasy seems real.

**Fairy tales are stories about good and evil.** These stories are all about black and white, good and bad, true and false. There are neither wimps in fairy tales nor any grays—nothing in between.

**The good characters are heroes and heroines.** They are handsome princes, beautiful princesses or someone who has never had an evil thought or done an evil deed. They would never do anything bad or selfish, even if their lives depended on their doing so. Fairy tales are always told from the point of view of the hero/heroine.

**The bad characters are villains.** They are ugly, cruel, mean-spirited, envious, and greedy witches, ogres, wolves, stepmothers, and monsters, who never had good, generous, kind, or loving thoughts in their lives. They always selfishly do anything to get what they want when they want it.

**The settings are always some imaginative kingdom far away where anything can, and does, happen.**

**Fairy tales often contain a journey of some kind.** The hero or heroine must travel through a deep, dark forest or across a wide, stormy sea full of dangers in order to do a good deed while the villain does everything in his/her power to stop it.

**Fairy tales are always told from the point of view of the hero/heroine.**

**Magic is often involved.**

**Good always triumphs over evil. The "good guy" wins by using his/her wits.**

Many familiar fairy tales may be found at these sites:

Grimm's Fairy Tales: **http://www.ul.cs.cmu.edu/books/GrimmFairy/**

Hans Christian Andersen's Fairy Tales: **http://www.math.technion.ac.il/~fl/Andersen/**

Legends Site Map: **http://www.legends.dm.net/sitemap.html**

7-9 Book Nook: **http://i-site.on.ca/booknook/79/index.html**

# FOCUS ON FAIRY TALE FLAWS

You can tell by reading about the characteristics of fairy tales on the previous page that they have a flaw. They are not fair. They present only one side of a story, and in our democratic society, this is far from right. Everyone is due his day in court. There are always two sides to every tale, even a fairy tale, and that is what this activity is all about. Do the following and tell the site from which you took the story.

**Choose three fairy tales from at least two different authors from one of the sites given and complete these statements about each.**

Who is the hero or heroine? _____

_____

Who is the "bad guy," the villain? _____

_____

What does the villain want from the hero or heroine? _____

_____

What does he/she do to try to get it? _____

_____

In what way does the hero/heroine outsmart the villain? _____

_____

What is the happy ending? _____

_____

From whose point of view was the story told? _____

_____

**Rewrite one of the stories you have just read.** In a democratic society, someone who commits a crime or does something against others has a right to tell his/her story from his/her own point of view. You are to tell the story from the point of view of the villain of this story. Tell the story of Cinderella from the point of view of the wicked stepmother or one of the stepsisters. Tell the story of Snow White from the point of view of the wicked queen or the story of the ugly duckling from the point of view of another baby duckling. Or choose a different story whose villain's side you'd like to take.

**Write your story on your word processor and submit it to this site.**

For Young Writers: **http://www.inkspot.com/young/**

# ANALYZING THE SHORT STORY

**Note to Teacher:** Because of the varying levels of reading ability in junior high, the sites below represent a wide range of ability levels to accommodate your students. Classic Short Stories and Complete Works of Edgar Allan Poe are most appropriate for students with above average reading skills, while the other three are appropriate for students of varying abilities. Choose the sites which best meet the needs of your students. Choose one story which you wish them to read or allow them to choose their own, depending on their level of literary maturity and your preference.

A short story or piece of short fiction contains three elements: setting, characters, and plot. It is also told from the point of view of one person. In this activity, students are to analyze one or more short stories to discover whether they meet the requirements of these elements. If a story does not have an element, the student should indicate that.

Read one short story you find on one of the sites below and identify the following:

Name of story _____

Author _____

Setting _____

Where? _____

When? _____

Main character _____

Other characters _____

Plot: _____

In this story _____ wanted _____

but _____ and _____

so _____ and _____

Finally, _____

_____

This story was told from _____'s point of view.

_____

Classic Short Stories: **http://www.bnl.com/shorts/**

Complete Works of Edgar Allan Poe: **gopher://wiretap.spies.com/11/Library/Classic/Poe**

The Boy Who Drew Cats: **http://www.ipl.org/youth/StoryHour/boycats/drewcats.html**

The Realist Wonder Society: **http://www.wondersociety.com/**

Dragon Stories: **http://www.users.interport.net/~fairrosa/dragon/**

# POETIC TERMS

Poetry has been written, listened to, and read for thousands of years. There are many different kinds of poetry. Some is funny, some sad. Some poems speak of love, others of anger. Some poems tell a story, others are about feelings. Some poems are like songs, and song lyrics are often a form of poetry.

To truly enjoy poetry, it helps to know some terms used when speaking of poetry. Go to this site and find the definitions of these poetry terms. Some of these terms are also used for other forms of literature besides poetry.

Literary Terms:

**http://www.clearcf.uvic.ca/writersguide/Pages/MasterToc.html#Literary Terms Alpha**

1. simile _____

2. metaphor _____

3. alliteration _____

4. ballad _____

5. blank verse _____

6. epic _____

7. free verse _____

8. heroic couplets _____

9. meter _____

10. imagery _____

11. onomatopoeia _____

12. ode _____

13. poetic justice _____

14. rhyme _____

15. sonnet _____

16. Which of these are terms for kinds of poems? _____

_____

# FIGURATIVE LANGUAGE IN POETRY—LANGSTON HUGHES

Imagery is essential to good poetry. Imagery is figurative language which includes similes and metaphors in ways which compare a thing to another by bringing up sensory images of what that thing is like. Similes compare things by using the words "as" or "like" while metaphors compare them by speaking as though the two things were the same. These two poems by Langston Hughes are examples of how similes and metaphors are used in a poem.

> **Hold fast to dreams**
> **for if dreams die**
> **life is a broken-winged bird**
> **that cannot fly.**
>
> **Hold fast to dreams**
> **for when dreams go**
> **life is a barren field**
> **frozen with snow**

In this poem, Hughes uses metaphors to compare things to one another. He writes of dreams as though they were actually something you could hold in your hand, of life without dreams as actually being a bird with a broken wing or a frozen field of snow.

> **What happens to a dream deferred?**
>
> **Does it dry up**
> **like a raisin in the sun?**
>
> **Or fester like a sore —**
> **and then run?**
>
> **Does it stink like rotten meat?**
> **Or crust and sugar over —**
> **like a syrupy sweet?**
>
> **Maybe it just sags**
> **like a heavy load.**
>
> **Or does it explode?**

In this poem, Hughes uses one simile after another to compare a dream which one has put off to a dried-up raisin, a festering sore, rotten meat, a syrupy sweet, a heavy load. Then he finishes with a metaphor—"does it explode?"—as though a dream were a tangible, material thing which could blow up.

# FIGURATIVE LANGUAGE IN POETRY— LANGSTON HUGHES *(cont.)*

Go to the following site

Langston Hughes: **http://www.nku.edu/~diesmanj/hughes.html** or

Langston Hughes: **http://www.math.buffalo.edu/~sww/poetry/hughes_langston.html**

Choose three poems by Langston Hughes.  Read them and name the ones you chose here.

_____

_____

On the back of this paper, list the similes and metaphors you find in each one of the poems.

Find the poem entitled, "The Negro Speaks of Rivers."  Read it carefully several times, letting its rhythm and language become familiar, and then answer these questions.

1.  This whole poem is, itself, a metaphor.  What is Hughes comparing in it? _____

    _____

2.  What does the river symbolize in this poem? _____

3.  Can you think of a reason why this might be so? _____

    _____

4.  What might the poet mean by, "I've known rivers"? _____

    _____

5.  What do you think the poet means by, "My soul has grown deep like the rivers"? _____

    _____

Go to these sites to learn about Langston Hughes, the poet and the man.  At Inference Find! type in the name, Langston Hughes, for many articles on the poet.  You may also learn about the Harlem Renaissance Hughes was a part of.

Inference Find: **http://www.infind.com/**

Langston Hughes: **http://www.encyclopedia.com/articles/06121.html**

Brief Biography of Langston Hughes: **http://www.cwrl.utexas.edu/~mmaynard/Hughes/hughes.htm**

Poems from the Planet Earth: **http://redfrog.norconnect.no/~poems/poets/langston_hughes.html**

Write a five-paragraph essay about Hughes and his poetry.  In your essay, tell how you believe Langston Hughes' poetry was influenced by his life and his racial heritage.

# SYMBOLS IN POETRY—ROBERT FROST

Poetry often contains symbolism; that is, the words in a poem often mean much more than the words by themselves. Symbols suggest a meaning apart from the mere words of a poem. What looks simple at first is more complicated. Certain words have gradually developed different meanings. Read this poem by Robert Frost.

**Nothing Gold Can Stay**

**Nature's first green is gold,**

**Her hardest hue to hold.**

**Her early leaf's a flower;**

**But only so an hour.**

**Then leaf subsides to leaf.**

**So Eden sank to grief,**

**So dawn goes down to day.**

Several words in this poem have multiple meanings. Gold, for example, often means illuminating and sacred, while green especially the first green of spring, means renewal and life. Dawn also means illumination and hope. Without knowing any more about symbolism, what do you think this poem means? Pay particular attention to the last line.

_____

_____

_____

Many of Robert Frost's poems have to do with the earth and with common, ordinary things which lead to self-discovery or acceptance. Use this online symbolism dictionary to find the symbolic meanings of these words from this poem and the next ones you are going to read.

Online Symbolism Dictionary: **http://www.umich.edu/~umfandsf/symbolismproject/symbolism.html**

1. leaf _____

2. journey _____

3. flower _____

4. forest (woods) _____

5. darkness _____

6. wind _____

7. bells _____

# SYMBOLS IN POETRY— ROBERT FROST *(cont.)*

Go to the poem at this site or find the poem in one of the other poetry sites. Print it.

The Road Not Taken: **http://www.kdi.com/~cdf/theroad.htm**

Robert Frost once said, "Every poem is a voyage of discovery. I go in to see if I can get out..."

Read, "The Road Not Taken," several times. Close your eyes and think about it.

1. What symbols do you find in the poem?_____

_____

2. Is the narrator describing a journey? _____

3. What did the narrator discover as a result of taking the road he chose? _____

_____

Go to this site and read, "Stopping by Woods on a Snowy Evening." Print it.

Stopping by Woods on a Snowy Evening: **http://www.kdi.com/~cdf/stopping.htm**

These two poems, "The Road Not Taken" and "Stopping by Woods on a Snowy Evening," are probably his most popular. Go to this site and read what Frost had to say about writing them.

Robert Frost on Poems: **http://www.libarts.sfasu.edu/Frost/PopPoems.html**

Discuss with your classmates the following: How did Robert Frost feel about these poems, and why did he write them? How do the symbols Frost used in these poems make the poems say more than just what seems to be happening on the surface of the poem? What do you think he was saying with these poems?

1. Go to one of the sites below and **find another poem by Robert Frost.** Memorize the poem and present it to the class.
2. **Illustrate the poem** you have chosen and make a poster of it. You may use paints, markers, make a collage, or use photographs.
3. **Write a poem** about something ordinary in your life. Study the rhyme scheme of "The Road Not Taken" and try to rhyme your poem in the same pattern with the same number of beats per line. Can you think of some symbols to use to make your poem more vivid?

Twentieth Century Poetry in English: **http://www.lit.kobe-u.ac.jp/~hishika/20c_poet.htm**

Poems from the Planet Earth: **http://redfrog.norconnect.no/poems/poets/robert_frost.html**

Robert Frost Poems: **http://www.pro-net.co.uk/home/catalyst/RF/poem1.html**

# READING SONNETS

Until the 1800s, an educated person memorized and recited classical poetry and wrote poetry. A person who could not do so was considered illiterate. A traditional poem, written by Shakespeare and many classical poets, is the **sonnet**. Go to this site to find sonnets by Shakespeare.

Complete Works of Shakespeare: **http://the-tech.mit.edu/Shakespeare/works.html**

Shakespeare wrote 154 sonnets which are considered some of the English-speaking world's most beautiful lines. "Elizabethan sonnet" refers to sonnets like those Shakespeare wrote. Most sonnets consisted of single, fourteen-line poems, but sometimes Elizabethan poets wrote entire narratives in sonnet form.

**A sonnet follows a set of rules.**

1. There are 14 lines in a sonnet.
    A. There are three sets of four lines called quatrains.
    B. There are two lines at the end called a couplet.

2. Each line contains ten syllables with every other syllable accented, usually beginning with the second syllable on each line.
   Example: When *in* the *chronicle* of *wasted time*

3. The sonnet has a formal rhyme scheme:
   abab
   cdcd
   efef
   gg

In this rhyme scheme the "a's" rhyme with each other, the "b's" rhyme with each other, and so forth.

4. The sonnet also has a *thematic structure*. Usually, the first two quatrains set up a problem, the third quatrain begins to answer the problems, and the ending couplet tries to solve the problem.

On the following page is a Shakespearean sonnet with the quatrains, couplet, and rhyme scheme identified for you. Can you identify the quatrains, couplets, and rhyme scheme?

**Bonus Points:** What are the problem and solution of the sonnet on following page?

# READING SONNETS *(cont.)*

| | |
|---|---|
| Those hours that with gentle work did frame | a |
| The lovely gaze where every eye doth dwell | b |
| Will play the tyrants to the very same | a |
| And that unfair which fairly doth excel. | b |
| For never-rusting time leads summer on | c |
| To hideous winter and confounds him there, | d |
| Sap checked with frost and lusty leaves quite gone, | c |
| Beauty o'er snowed and bareness everywhere. | d |
| Then, were not summer's distillation left, | e |
| A liquid prisoner pent in walls of glass | f |
| Beauty's effect with beauty were bereft, | e |
| Nor it, nor no remembrance what it was. | f |
| But flowers distilled, though they with winter meet, | g |
| Leese but their show. Their substance still lives sweet. | g |

Shakespeare was not the only poet who wrote sonnets, of course, since writing them was part of being educated. One of the most famous writers of sonnets was Elizabeth Barrett Browning, who wrote, Sonnets from the Portuguese. Go to this site and find a sonnet written by Browning. Complete the following about the sonnets you have read.

Elizabeth Barrett Browning:
**http://www.inform.umd.edu/EdRes/Topic/WomensStudies/ReadingRoom/Poetry/BarrettBrowning/**

1. Name of the Browning sonnet you read. _____

2. How is the Browning sonnet like the Shakespeare sonnet above? _____

   _____

   _____

3. How is the Browning sonnet different from the one by Shakespeare? _____

   _____

   _____

4. Find a Shakespeare or Browning sonnet from either of these sites. Read the sonnet over several times, read it aloud, and then memorize it and present it to the class.

5. Try to write a sonnet. What is the most difficult part about writing one?

# SONG LYRICS AS POETRY

Many people never think of song lyrics as being poetry, but they often are. One of the oldest English forms of poetry is the **ballad**, which was really a song which told a story and was sung around the countryside by a minstrel. The minstrel may have written the lyrics himself, or he may have learned them from another minstrel. Many popular and country-western songs are ballads, as are folk songs. And there are other song lyrics which are also kinds of poems.

**Go to this site with the entire list of Muppet songs and find lyrics to "The Rainbow Connection." Print the lyrics.**

Muppet Songs: **http://www.cs.unc.edu/~arthur/muppet-songs.html**

1. On the back of this paper, list some reasons to call this song a poem.

2. What, if any, symbols do you see in these lyrics?_____

3. What do you think is the "rainbow connection"? _____

_____

**Go to this site and find the lyrics to the top ten songs.** List the first three. Print the lyrics to the one you like best. Are any of these lyrics poems? List your reasons for your answer.

International Lyrics Server: **http://www.lyrics.ch/**

_____

_____

_____

**Go to this site and find the lyrics for the songs in the Disney movie you like best of the ones shown.** Print the lyrics. Which movie song is your favorite?

Disney Movie Lyrics: **http://thoth.stetson.edu/users/Bill_Sawyer/Disney/Lyrics.html**

Write a one-page essay comparing and contrasting two of the lyrics you found. Then explore the lyrics on one of these sites. Do you know any of these songs?

Lyrics Library-Bing Crosby: **http://www.mathematik.uni-ulm.de/paul/lyrics/bingcrosby/**

The Sinatra Songbook: **http://www.vex.net/~buff/sinatra/song_index.html**

Elton John Lyrics: **http://ej.kylz.com/songs/index.html**

# STORYTELLING IN POETRY—EDGAR ALLAN POE

Edgar Allan Poe was a storyteller. He wrote strange tales of tell-tale hearts beating under the floor and guilty consciences, of black cats and grand, bizarre parties full of reds and blacks and swirling images. He also wrote poetry, and many of his poems told stories. "The Raven" is one of those poems which is a story. Find this poem at this site. Print it. Poe used a huge vocabulary in his works. Use the dictionary site to find the meanings of some of the words in "The Raven."

Complete Collection of Poems by Edgar Allan Poe (+ biography):
**http://www.rit.edu/~exb1874/mine/poe/poe_ind.html**

WWWebster Dictionary: **http://www.m-w.com/dictionary**

1. surcease _____

2. obeisance _____

3. mien _____

4. decorum _____

5. ebony _____

6. countenance _____

7. discourse _____

8. desolate _____

9. respite _____

10. ominous _____

11. pallid _____

12. melancholy _____

13. placid _____

14. relevancy _____

15. censer _____

**Bonus points:** How many of these words can you write into a paragraph? **Hint:** Many of them are adjectives. Use them to describe nouns.

# STORYTELLING IN POETRY—EDGAR ALLAN POE *(cont.)*

**A. Read this stanza of "The Raven" aloud** carefully.  Notice the way in which Poe rhymed the poem.

> Once upon a midnight dreary, while I pondered, weak and weary,
> Over many a quaint and curious volume of forgotten lore—
> While I nodded, nearly napping, suddenly there came a tapping,
> As of someone gently rapping, rapping at my chamber door.
> 'Tis some visitor,' I muttered, 'tapping at my chamber door—
> Only this and nothing more.'

The rhyme scheme is complicated, isn't it?  You have words rhyming not only at the ends of lines but within the lines, as well.  Now read the second stanza and underline the rhyming words.  Better yet, color the ones which rhyme with each other with colored markers; use the same color for each rhyming pattern.

> Ah, distinctly I remember it was in the bleak December,
> And each separate dying ember wrought its ghost upon the floor.
> Eagerly I wished the morrow;—vainly I had sought to borrow
> From my books surcease of sorrow—sorrow for the lost Lenore—
> For the rare and radiant maiden whom the angels name Lenore—
> Nameless here forevermore.

Is the rhyme scheme in this stanza the same as the one in the first stanza? _____

What ending sound continues through both stanzas?_____

**B. Poe repeats certain sounds.  Circle the words which he repeats.**  Why do you think he does this?

_____

**C. Why do you think the raven keeps saying, "Nevermore"?** _____

**D. Read the rest of the poem.**  Listen to its rhythm.  What do you think gives the poem its rhythm?

_____

**E. "The Raven" tells a story.**  Rewrite the story of the poem in prose.  Is the story as effective in prose as in poetry?

**F. Read another poem by Poe from one of these sites.**  Does it tell a story, too?

Edgar Allan Poe Poems: **http://triton.pc.uni-koein.de/Poe/**

Works of Poe: **http://www.comnet.ca/~forrest/works.html**

The Poe Decoder: **http://www.poedecoder.com/**

# POETRY STRIPS

This activity is something of a reverse to the one in which students put their lines together to form new poetry. In this activity, the students will take the lines of a poem already written and taken apart and try to put it back together. It works best with narrative poetry, although you could use it with other forms of poetry, as well.

## Teacher Preparation:

1. Gather several narrative poems from different poets. The poems of Robert Frost, "The Owl and the Pussycat," by Edward Lear, and the poems of Edgar Allan Poe work well for this activity and may be printed off free at these sites.

   Twentieth Century Poetry in English: **http://www.lit.kobe-u.ac.jp/~hishika/20c_poet.htm**

   Poems from the Planet Earth: **http://redfrog.norconnect.no/poems/poets/robert_frost.html**

   Robert Frost Poems: **http://www.pro-net.co.uk/home/catalyst/RF/poem1.html**

   Edgar Allan Poe Poems: **http://triton.pc.uni-koeln.de/Poe/**

   Works of Poe: **http://www.comnet.ca/~forrest/works.html**

   Edward Lear, Nonsense songs: **http://www2.pair.com/mgraz/Lear/ns/index.html**

2. Being sure to keep the strips of each poem separate from the strips of other poems, print the poem, or poems, to use. Cut the poem(s) into strips with one line to each strip.

3. Place the strips into a box and mix them up.

4. Have small cooperative groups work together to put a poem back together based on their ideas about how the narration would develop.

5. After a group has reassembled its poem, send them to the appropriate Internet site to determine how successful their reassembly was.

This activity may be used successfully with two or more poems.

# WRITING POETRY—CINQUAIN

Cinquains are poems of five lines. They were first written by an American named Adelaide Crapsey. She was impressed by the simplicity and beauty of the Japanese haiku, and determined to create a poem in English which was as simple and effective as haiku. A great American poet, Carl Sandburg, liked what she created so much, he wrote a poem about her and her poems.

Like haiku, a Cinquain has a strict structure of lines and syllables per line. The usual way to write one is like this:

> Line 1: One word which serves as the first line of the poem and its title
>
> Line 2: Two words describing the title
>
> Line 3: Three words showing action by the title
>
> Line 4: Two words conveying a feeling about the title
>
> Line 5: Another word for the title

The numbers of syllables in the lines are first line, two syllables; second line, four syllables; third line, six syllables; fourth line, eight syllables, last line, two or three syllables. The subject does not have to be of nature, as does the haiku. It can be anything.

Visit the sites below. Read cinquains which have been written by other students, and then write a cinquain of your own. It will be shaped like this.

_____

_____

_____

_____

_____

Cinquains and Diamantes: **http://kidswriting.miningco.com/library/weekly/aa112097.htm**

Willis School Poetry Club-Cinquain: **http://www.aces.k12.ct.us/classweb/ansonia/CIN.HTM**

# WRITING POETRY—HAIKU

**Haiku** is a traditional form of poetry written for hundreds of years in Japan, and it has become very popular all over the world. Haiku is easy to write, but traditional haiku follows some strict rules.

1. There are 17 syllables in each verse.
2. The first and third lines have five syllables each.
3. The second line has seven syllables.
4. Each verse must identify a season of the year: winter, spring, summer, fall.
5. The poem must paint a picture of nature.

At the sites below you will find directions for writing haiku, and you will also find examples of haiku written by students. Go to those sites and read the haiku other students have written.

**Write a haiku with four verses.** Have the first verse be of winter, the second of spring, the third of summer, and the fourth of fall.

Haiku—Creative Writing for Kids: **http://kidswriting.miningco.com/library/weekly/aa100297.htm**

Willis School Poetry Club-Haiku: **http://www.aces.k12.ct.us/classweb/ansonia/HAI.HTM**

# HANG-IT-ALL-HAIKU CENTER

We all have poetry in us, but sometimes it's difficult to get it all together at one time. Sometimes the cooperation of students can lead to a combination of lines which make poetry.

**Teacher preparation:** For this activity, the teacher needs to set aside a special place on the bulletin board which is easily accessible to all students. Nearby on a table or desk set aside for the purpose, lay out the following:

> strips of paper $^1/_2$ inch by 4-6 inches (1.3 cm by 10-15 cm)
>
> fine-line or medium markers
>
> pushpins, thumbtacks, or cellophane tape

Before turning the students loose at the center, send them to these sites about haiku. Have them read other student-written haiku.

Haiku—Creative Writing for Kids: **http://kidswriting.miningco.com/library/weekly/aa100297.htm**

Willis School Poetry Club-Haiku: **http://www.aces.k12.ct.us/classweb/ansonia/HAI.HTM**

Discuss the purpose of haiku—to write a poem about something in nature. Discuss the structure of haiku—a line of five syllables, followed by a line of seven syllables and then another line of five syllables.

**Place above the center these instructions:**

1. Write one line of five syllables or one line of seven syllables on each strip of paper.

2. Read other lines written by other students. When you see one which would go with a line you have written, stick the two lines up on the bulletin board together. Be sure that you place the lines in the format for a haiku poem.

Leave the center up for a given length of time —two weeks might be a good length of time. Allow students to contribute lines to the board as they occur in their minds. Encourage them to discuss the lines and possible arrangements into haiku.

As a culminating activity, place the haiku, formed this way, into a class poetry book.

# WRITING LIMERICKS

Limericks are poems with five lines which usually make little sense, and they are some of the most humorous poems of all. Sometimes they are written as having four lines with the third and fourth combining into one line with a rhyme at the end of the line and in the middle. For this activity, we'll use the five-line format. This is a limerick:

> There once was a student in school
>
> Who followed a practical rule:
>
> She hid all her books
>
> In crannies and nooks
>
> Without even losing her cool.

Edward Lear was one of the most famous of limerick writers. His limericks do not make sense, and they are not supposed to do so, which is the reason they are called nonsense poems. But they are fun to read and recite. Read some of the limericks of Edward Lear's at his home page below, and then go to the other limerick sites and notice the structure of the limerick. The structure is how the poem is put together: its shape, its rhythm, and its rhyme pattern.

The rhyme pattern for a limerick is aabba. If you look at the limerick above, you'll see that the first two lines rhyme with each other (a,a), then the third and fourth line rhyme with each other (b,b), and the last line rhymes with the first two (a). If you will go to the Limerick Discussion Page below, you'll learn other things about the limerick and its beat and rhythm. Note the number of syllables in each line and their relationship to each other. After you study the way in which the limerick is structured, write one of your own. This form will help you structure your limerick. Try stringing several verses of limericks together for a longer poem.

_____

_____

_____

_____

_____

**Submit your limerick to one of the sites on page for publication.**

Edward Lear Homepage: **http://www2.pair.com/mgraz/Lear/index.html**

Limerick Discussion Page: **http://www.sfu.ca/~finley/discussion.html**

Semantic Rhyming Dictionary: **http://www.link.cs.cmu.edu/dougb/rhyme-doc.html**

Nonsense Links: **http://www2.pair.com/mgraz/Lear/ll.html**

# PUBLISH YOUR WRITING ON THE INTERNET

Most people who write like to share what they have written with others. The Internet is a great place for sharing poetry and other creative writing. Check out these sites to determine whether they will publish your writing or allow you to send it to others.

1. **Create a postcard to e-mail to your friends and relatives.** At these sites you choose your background and a picture for your card and write a message. It is a great way to send poetry and short pieces of writing. Some of your choices even have animation. Choose one of the poems you have written. Copy the poem and paste it in the message box of your postcard site, then e-mail it.

   Digital Postcard **http://www.all-yours.net/postcard/dp.html**

   Electric Postcards: **http://postcards.www.media.mit.edu/Postcards**

   The Cyber Greeting Collection: **http://www.surfme.com/cgc/nonframe.shtml**

2. **Share your poetry with students from around the world.** These sites specialize in student poetry. Read the rules first and then submit.

   Positively Poetry: **http://advicom.net/~e-mdia/kv/poetry1.html**

   Poetry Pals, Internet Poetry Publishing Project:
   **http://www.geocities.com/EnchantedForest/5165/**

3. **Enter a writing contest.** These sites have contests where you may enter your creative writing or poetry and compete with other student writers.

   Writing Contests for Kids: **http://kidswriting.miningco.com/msub40.htm**

   Send a Story & Win a Prize: **http://www.ozemail.com.au/~oban/index.html**

4. **Creative writing opportunities:** At these sites you will find other opportunities for you to share your writing with students far away from you.

   Creative Writing Opportunities: **http://kidswriting.miningco.com/msub40.htm**

   For Young Writers: **http://www.inkspot.com/young/**

   KidPub: **http://www.kidpub.org/kidpub/howto.html**

## Good writing to you!

# RELEASE FOR ELECTRONICALLY DISPLAYED STUDENT WORK

Dear Parents/Guardians,

We are excited to let you know that our class will be publishing our work on a portion of the Internet called the World Wide Web. This means that anyone in the world who has access to the Web will be able to view your child's work. The potential audience is in the millions.

Your signature below acknowledges permission for such work to be published on the World Wide Web.

Yours truly,


Classroom Teacher

_____ My child's work, which may be accompanied by his/her first name, may be electronically displayed and produced.

_____ My child's work, which may not be accompanied by his/her first name, may be electronically displayed and produced.

_____ Photographs of my child, which may be accompanied by his/her first name, may be electronically displayed and produced.

_____ Photographs of my child, which may not be accompanied by his/her first name, may be electronically displayed and produced.

I hereby give the above permission and release from any liability resulting from or connected with the publication of such work.

Child's name _____

Teacher _____

Parent or guardian signature _____

Date _____

# PRODUCE A RADIO NEWS PROGRAM

Before the advent of television, radio and newspapers were where most people in Europe, Asia, and the United States got their information about what was happening in the world. During World War II, many people listened to radio newscasts avidly. Many of their friends and relatives and their families were involved in the fighting, and they wanted to know the status of the war in places where loved ones were.

Some newscasters became famous, their voices well-known to millions of people, and some went on to become television anchors or commentators. In some parts of the world, radio is still more important than television, and many people leave their car radios turned on to keep caught up on the news of the day while driving to and from their jobs or wherever they need to go.

Writing for a radio newscast is a little different from writing for television news. Writing for radio involves writing for only the spoken voice, while when writing for television, the acting ability and appearance of the newscasters are as important as what they say. Some radio newscasters who also became television newscasters include these names which may be familiar to you:

**Chet Huntley**

**David Brinkley**

**Edward R. Murrow**

**Walter Cronkite**

Using the links on the following page, complete these activities about radio and television newscasting.

1. **Research the life and career of one of the above newscasters,** one of your own choosing, or one from this list.

    **Dan Rather**

    **Tom Brokaw**

    **Peter Jennings**

    **Connie Chung**

Prepare a brief report on this person to present to the class. Determine whether this newscaster has received any awards or written any books and, if so, name the books or awards. How did this person first go into radio/television? Did he/she study news broadcasting in college? Is there any special piece of news for which he/she is most famous for having been the one to cover the story?

2. **Complete a history of radio and television broadcasting.** Include specific dates of the first radio and television news broadcasts, and cite some statistics which show how the industry has grown during the years since it began.

# PRODUCE A RADIO NEWS PROGRAM *(cont.)*

3. **Research a specific radio or television news agency.** Some of the largest in the United States are:

ABC

NBC

CBS

CNN

PBS

NPR

FOX

When did the news agency begin? Is there anything which distinguishes this news agency from the others?

4. **Go online to one of the news agencies** listed below or to one which isn't listed here. Read the day's news contained on the site and choose one of the events covered. Write a news account of that event. Record that account on a tape recorder as it would be broadcast on a radio newscast. Play your recording for the class.

5. **Choose an event or happening at school which interests you.** It could be a sports event, a spelling bee, the honor roll, or something special which one of your classmates has done. Write a report of the event.

6. **Present a daily or weekly news program for the school.** After completing any or all of the above activities, extend the activity into a daily or weekly news program which you present for the school over the public address system or intercom. Develop regular features to cover each week, such as sports events, scholarship events, awards and honors won by students, or special achievements of individual students or teachers. Ask the principal to give a weekly editorial on a subject of interest to all the people at the school.

Radio Days—News: **http://www.otr.com/news.html**

Memories of Early Television: **http://www.geocities.com/TelevisionCity/Set/1459**

Broadcasting: **http://www.encyclopedia.com/articles/01882.htm**

The Museum of Television and Radio: **http://www.mtr.org/**

ABC.com: **http://www.abc.com/**

CNN Interactive: **http://www.cnn.com/**

NBC's Home on the Web: **http://www.nbc.com/**

# THAT WAS THE DAY, OR YEAR, THAT WAS

Did you ever wonder what the world was like on your birthday a hundred years ago? or what happened that was important 547 years ago? or which people were around on the day you were born? or anything about the people who did significant things during the time that Julius Caesar lived, or Cleopatra, or Romeo and Juliet, or George Washington?

It's possible to learn many of these things just by going online. You'll need access to an online encyclopedia such as the one below or access to the history channel, and a knowledge of how to write an essay for this activity. You can obtain all these from the three sites below. You will also need a word processor for writing your essay.

## Do one of the following:

1. **Choose a year which interests you.** Search the main events and people of that year in the online encyclopedia. Print any pictures or charts you find connected to those events and people to use as illustrations for your essay. Study *How to Write a History Essay* and then write an essay based on the information you have obtained from the encyclopedia. Be sure to have an introductory paragraph, three paragraphs to form the body of your essay, and a concluding paragraph which ties together all the information you obtained. Write your essay on the word processor, and illustrate it with the pictures and/or charts you have been able to find. Turn in your essay.

To see a sample report that was created by simply typing in the year 1742, go to

Encarta Advanced Search: **http://w3.arizona.edu/~susd/1742.htm**

2. **Choose a date which interests you.** It could be your birthday or that of one of your parents or grandparents, or it could be any date which you consider significant for some reason. Search *This Day in History* at the *History Channel* site. What people were important on that day? Were there any significant events which happened then? Print off any pictures or charts to use as illustrations for your essay. Study *How to Write a History Essay,* then write an essay based on the information you have obtained from the History Channel. Be sure to have an introductory paragraph, three paragraphs to form the body of your essay, and a concluding paragraph which ties all the information you obtained together. Write your essay on the word processor and illustrate it with the pictures and/or charts you have been able to find. Turn in your essay.

A Year in History: Encarta Advanced Search: **http://encarta.msn.com/find/advancedfind.asp**

This Day in History: **http://www.historychannel.com/today/**

How to Write a History Essay: **http://kanga.pvhs.chico.k12.ca.us/~bsilva/ib/hstess.html**

# WHAT IS AN ESSAY?

An essay is a short written composition about a topic.  Sometimes essays are called theme papers, term papers, or simply compositions.  There are many kinds of essays, and in your school career you will probably be asked to write a number of each.  Using the sites below, find an explanation of the purpose of each of the following essays.  Write a brief definition of each.

1. definition essay _____

2. evaluation essay _____

3. personal essay _____

4. narrative essay _____

5. comparison and contrast essay _____

   _____

6. classification essay _____

7. literary essay _____

8. essay exam _____

Essays may ask you to demonstrate a process of some kind, describe a subject, persuade the reader to believe or do something, review a literary work or study, describe a research project, or react to a question.  You need your best writing skills for any essay.  The writing centers below are excellent sites for you to refer to when writing any sort of essay.  Each emphasizes a little different aspect of writing, but all emphasize good writing.  Bookmark them or put them in your favorite places for use in the future.

5-Paragraph Essay: **http://members.aol.com/AACTchAndy/edu/essayform.html**

Basic Guide to Essay Writing: **http://members.aol.com/lklivngstn/essay/**

Essay Builder: **http://www2.actden.com/writ_den/tips/essay/index.thm**

LEO Write Place Catalog: **http://leo.stcloud.msus.edu/catalogue.html**

Paradigm Writing Assistant: **http://www.idbsu.edu/english/cguilfor/paradigm/**

University of Victoria Writer's Guide: The Essay:
**http://www.clearcf.uvic.ca/writersguide/Pages/EssayToc.html**

Purdue Online Writing Lab: **http://owl.english.purdue.edu/**

# HOW DO YOU DECIDE WHAT TO WRITE?

When your teacher gives you a definite subject to write about, you are in luck because the most difficult part about writing an essay can be deciding on your topic. Can you imagine the following scene?

Your class has just finished reading *To Kill a Mockingbird.* Your teacher announces in class, "Your assignment is to write a 500-word essay on *To Kill A Mockingbird."* Period!

You have been given no specific instructions. You have no idea what to write. You're not even sure what the main themes of the book are. This would be panic time, right? Fortunately, teachers are usually much more precise about what they want from their students. Whether the teacher does or does not give you an exact subject, however, you need to narrow down your possibilities and focus on a main idea for your essay.

1. Go to Paradigm Online Writing Assistant and find the section entitled "Discovering What to Write." Your assignment is to write a literary essay entitled, "The Most Important Theme(s) in _____ (the book or story you have just read in class)"

   What does "Choosing a Subject" tell you to do first?_____

   _____

2. What is "freewriting," and how will it help you get started on your essay?_____

   _____

3. Why is it important for you to observe details? _____

   _____

4. What sorts of details should you be thinking about when writing about a character in the story?

   _____

5. Write a five-paragraph essay on the most important themes in your book or story. Narrow your themes down to no more than two or three. Follow the steps suggested in Paradigm and the steps for writing a five-paragraph essay in another site.

Paradigm Writing Assistant: **http://www.idbsu.edu/english/cguilfor/paradigm/**

5-Paragraph Essay: **http://members.aol.com/AACTchAndy/edu/essayform.html**

LEO Write Place Catalog: **http://leo.stcloud.msus.edu/catalogue.html**

# WRITING A THESIS STATEMENT

A **thesis statement** is the beginning sentence or paragraph of an essay. It introduces the main idea of the essay, and if it is good, it will grab the interest of your reader and tell him why your topic is important. A good thesis statement is limited to the topic about which you are going to write and leads toward points you wish to make later. Go to this site and study examples of good and bad thesis statements.

LEO Thesis Statement: **http://leo.stcloud.msus.edu/acadwrite/thesistatement.html**

List five things a thesis statement does:

1. _____

2. _____

3. _____

4. _____

5. _____

List four things a thesis statement does not do:

6. _____

7. _____

8. _____

9. _____

**Change the following into good thesis statements:**

There is too much pollution in our air.

The thesis of this paper is the way cars are causing too much air pollution.

Education in a technological society

Problems of American education

Shakespeare wrote many plays, but there is some disagreement about whether he wrote them all himself.

University of Victoria Writer's Guide: The Essay:
**http://www.clearcf.uvic.ca/writersguide/Pages/EssayToc.html**

Purdue Online Writing Lab: **http://owl.english.purdue.edu/**

Essay Builder: **http://www2.actden.com/writ_den/tips/essay/index.htm**

# WRITING A DEFINITION ESSAY

An essay is usually written to answer a question of some sort. The question may be one your teacher asks you, or it may be one you ask yourself. A **definition essay** will try to answer a question such as "What is an X?" or "Define X," but it will do more than just give a dictionary definition of the subject. Find two descriptions of a definition essay from the sites on the previous page and answer these questions.

1. What is the first thing your definition essay will do? _____

   _____

2. It is sometimes said a writer should write about what he knows best. How might this be true when writing a definition essay? _____

   _____

3. Abstract words such as patriotism, love, beauty, and justice are difficult subjects to write about. Why is this true? _____

   _____

4. List at least five things which help define an object or term thoroughly. _____

   _____

   _____

   _____

5. Choose one of the following topics or a topic of your own and write a 250-word definition essay.

   **Define an effective teacher.**

   **What is the Internet?**

   **What is a good book?**

   **Define a happy home.**

   **What makes for the best classroom?**

   **Define a loyal friend.**

# WRITING AN ESSAY EXAM

Writing an **essay exam** is like writing any other essay with two major differences: your time is limited, and you are not able to revise. In addition, you may not know the exact topic ahead of time. Sometimes a teacher will prepare you before the day of the exam by giving you sample topics to study or even the precise topic. Other times, you will know only in a general way what you will be expected to write.

What this means is that you must take the first few minutes of the time you will have for writing your essay to plan what you will write. Before you do anything else, you need to make sure you understand the question being asked. You do not want to spend all your time writing an essay which answers a question different from the one being asked. The teacher wants to know what you know about a given topic, so you need to concentrate on that topic. Go to this site and to the section on essay exams to study the general guides you need to have about writing essay exams.

University of Victoria Writer's Guide: The Essay:
**http://www.clearcf.uvic.ca/writersguide/Pages/EssayToc.html**

An essay exam can take the form of any other kind of essay: evaluative, compare and contrast, definition, narrative, personal, literary, etc. Again, you must read the question carefully. You will have a good idea of exactly what form your essay should take, if you understand the question and answer accordingly. Teachers use certain key words which are clues to the form your essay should take. Go to this site to learn how to recognize key words in essay exam questions.

Purdue Online Writing Lab: **http://owl.english.purdue.edu/**

Once you understand the question, you need to plan your essay. Review the structure of the basic essay at the sites below. Learn this structure so well you automatically go on auto-pilot when writing any kind of essay.

Now that you understand the question, write a brief outline for your essay on the inside cover of your blue book, or wherever the teacher allows you to do so. Write your thesis statement based on the question. Begin writing only after your outline is complete.

**Write a practice essay exam which answers the following question: Which would you rather own—a compact car or a full-size car?** (How can you tell this will be a compare-contrast essay?)

5-Paragraph Essay: **http://members.aol.com/AACTchAndy/edu/essayform.html**

Basic Guide to Essay Writing: **http://members.aol.com/lklivngstn/essay/**

Essay Builder: **http://www2.actden.com/writ_den/tips/essay/index.htm**

# WRITING A COMPARISON AND CONTRAST ESSAY

The most useful kind of essay of them all is probably the **comparison** and **contrast** essay. Any time you have two things to write about, you can use it. In a comparison and contrast essay you say how two things are alike and how they're different.

To help you line up all the information you have and which you want to include in your essay, it helps to divide a piece of paper into three columns. At the top of the first column, put "A," or the name of the first thing. At the top of the last column, put "B," or the name of the second thing. In the middle column, put A and B. In the first column, list all the ways in which "A" is unique. In the last column, list all the ways in which "B" is unique, and in the center column list all the characteristics "A" and "B" share. Now you're all lined up to write a comparison and contrast essay.

Go to this site:

LEO Comparison/Contrast Essays: **http://leo.stcloud.msus.edu/acadwrite/comparcontrast.html**

List the four different ways of writing a comparison/contrast essay.

1. _____

2. _____

3. _____

4. _____

How could you use compare/contrast besides as an essay topic?

_____

Use sites above and below to help you compare and contrast one of these pairs of topics. Write a 250-word essay.

> **public and private schools**
>
> **baseball and football**
>
> **the short story and the novel**
>
> **Romeo and Juliet**
>
> **movies and television**
>
> **CDs and live entertainment**
>
> **surfing and skateboarding**
>
> **U.S. President and British Prime Minister**

Guide to Grammar and Writing: **http://webster.commnet.edu/HP/pages/darling/grammar.htm**

# WRITING A NARRATIVE ESSAY

A **narrative** essay tells a story. It may do so to entertain, or it may do so to inform, and it is not written in quite the same way as a formal essay. Go to this site and take a path through the section called **Principles of Composition**. Under **Patterns of Composition**, see **The Personal Essay** and **Narrative and Descriptive Essay**.

Guide to Grammar and Writing: **http://webster.commnet.edu/HP/pages/darling/grammar.htm**

1. What is the purpose of an essay? _____

2. What must you not do when writing a narrative essay? _____
_____

**Read the essay "My Watch: An Instructive Little Tale" by Mark Twain.**

3. What is the point of Twain's essay? _____
_____

4. How is there movement in the essay? _____

5. This essay was published almost a century ago. How would the paragraphs most likely be spaced today?

_____

_____

_____

Go these writing sites and the punctuation of sentences section in the one above. Learn how to use quotation marks. Write a narrative essay on one of these subjects or one of your own. Include direct quotations in your essay.

> **The day the car engine died**
> **Taking my little brother to the movie**
> **The night the lights went out**
> **Babysitting: The Wrong Way to Do It**
> **Surfing the Web on a Search Engine**

Craft of Writing: **http://www.inkspot.com/craft/**

Sentence Punctuation Patterns: **http://owl.english.purdue.edu/Files/2.html**

# WRITING A LITERARY ESSAY

A **literary** essay is an essay in which you write about how a piece of literature is put together (structured) and what it means. It may be almost entirely your own opinion backed by what you read in the work, but it will be more specific than a review. It may be a combination of what you think and what others have said about it, and when this is true, it becomes more of a research paper.

In writing a literary essay, certain literary terms are frequently used. It's important to be precise, so your reader will know exactly what you mean.

Go to this site and follow the path to **General Writing Concerns**. Then scroll down to **Writing about Fiction**. Find the definitions of the following literary terms.

Outline of Documents at the Purdue Writing Lab:
**http://owl.english.purdue.edu/writers/by-topic.html**

1. characterization _____

2. conflict _____

3. dialogue _____

4. imagery _____

5. point of view _____

6. symbol _____

7. tone_____

**Now go to this site and scroll down to "The Lottery" by Shirley Jackson.**

Classic Short Stories: **http://www.bnl.com/shorts/**

Read the story, then on a separate sheet of paper, list examples from the story of the above literary terms.

Using this paper as notes, write a short essay detailing how this story illustrates one of the terms. Use examples from the story to show what you mean. If you still need help constructing the essay, go to either this site or the Purdue site above. Publish your essay on Book Nook.

University of Victoria Writer's Guide: The Literary Essay
**http://www.clearcf.uvic.ca/writersguide/Pages/LiteraryEssay.html**

Book Nook: **http://i-site.on.ca/booknook.html**

# WRITING A CHARACTER ANALYSIS

Of the three main elements of a story—setting, characters and plot—the characters may be the most critical to a story, for what is setting without the characters moving around in it? What is plot unless the reader can see the characters as real and care what happens to them or what they do?

An author shows a character in several ways. She shows him in action, doing things which are "characteristic" of the kind of person he is. She allows the reader to listen in on what he says and how he says it. She allows the reader to hear what other characters say about him and sometimes allows the reader to listen in on his thoughts. The author sometimes comes right out and tells the reader what kind of person he is. The reader who gets to know a character wants to read on in the story to learn what will happen to him, what he will do, where his life will lead.

A well-written character will have strengths and weaknesses like other human beings. It's hard to relate to a character who does not show his different sides as a person. Without different sides to his personality, he becomes a stick figure, a straw man, someone without a soul. The reader will simply say, "Who cares?" and stop reading.

What are the things a reader wants to know about a character? Usually, he wants to know these things:

- Why does the character say what he says?
- Why does the character do what he does?
- What does he consider important?
- What will he do in a certain situation?

Go to this site to learn more about what to look for in a character in order to write a character analysis.

How to Write a Character Analysis: **http://members.aol.com/AACTchAndy/edu/charanaly.html**

According to the information on this site, what are the things you must look for when writing a character analysis? Explain in your own words.

1. _____

_____

2. _____

_____

3. _____

_____

# WRITING A CHARACTER ANALYSIS *(cont.)*

Go to this site, and scroll down to "Bellflower," by Guy de Maupassant. If you wish and you have a printer, print out the story. Read the story on- or offline.

Classic Short Stories: **http://www.bnl.com/shorts/**

Who is the narrator of this story? _____

Who is the main character? _____

Describe her appearance. _____

Why does the narrator tell us about her? _____

What is her main physical feature? _____

What is she to the boy?_____

Given what you're told about the main character by the narrator and by the doctor in the story, what can you tell about her in terms of the three things you are to look for when doing a character analysis?

Why did she live the way she lived? _____

_____

How can you tell? _____

What was important to her? _____

_____

How can you tell? _____

How did she react when the young man told her to hide? _____

_____

Do you agree that she was punished for what she did? _____

_____

Using the instructions at the site on the previous page, write a five paragraph character analysis of Mother Clochette.

# WRITING A BIOGRAPHY

You will be asked to provide biographical information many times in your school career: as part of book reports and reviews, as written biographies, and as part of literary essays. Thanks to the Internet, you have the world of information at your fingertips. There are few major artists, writers, historical figures, and poets whom you will not find some place. So just how are you going to write a biography?

This site is an excellent one which gives you step-by-step instructions on writing a biography. Go to it and find the following information about how to write a biography.

Biography Maker: **http://www.bham.wednet.edu/bio/biomak2.htm**

**What are the five steps toward writing a good biography?**

1. _____

2. _____

3. _____

4. _____

5. _____

**Identify and explain the six traits of effective writing.**

1. _____

2. _____

3. _____

4. _____

5. _____

6. _____

Here are some sites where you will find help in researching the topic of your biography. Also remember the encyclopedia and search engines for information.

Biographies: **http://members.aol.com/AACTchrOz/biosculture.html**

Biography.com/find: **http://www.biography.com/find/find.html**

WIC Biography Index: **http://www.wic.org/bio/idex_bio.htm**

Women in American History: **http://women.eb.com./women/ind_articles.html**

People in Science: **http://www.windows.umich.edu/people/people.html**

# WRITING A BIOGRAPHY *(cont.)*

Go to this site.

World History Chart: **http://users/uniserve.com/~andreasn/chart/chart.html**

Choose from this chart or from another source one person for your biography. Notice that the people are shown in terms of their having done something significant in one of several different fields, including the sciences, the arts, and politics. They are also shown on a time line as having lived between 1500 and 1997, and the term usually given to the "age" in which they lived is shown on the blue bar running through the inner part of the chart.

Before beginning your biography, fill in this information about your subject.

Subject of biography_____

Time during which person lived (lives) _____

Your reasons for choosing this person _____

_____

How is this person significant?_____

Sources of information you will use in your biography. (Choose at least three, including one encyclopedia.)

_____

_____

_____

_____

When writing your biography, be sure to name the sources for your information in a bibliography. Go to these sites to learn how to cite information taken from the Internet.

How to Cite Electronic Resources: **http://www.williams.edu:803/library/library.www/cite.html**

MLA Citation Examples: **http://www.hcc.hawaii.edu/education/hcc/library/mlahcc.html**

Citing Electronic Sources: **http://owl.english.purdue.edu/Files/110.html**

# WRITING A RESEARCH PAPER

**Writing a research** essay can be a daunting project for someone just beginning to get into the academic classes of junior and senior high school. It's easy for a student to panic each time a teacher says, "Write a research paper. One third of your grade will be based on this paper."

**What do you do?** First look at some things not to do.

**The first thing *not* to do is panic.** There is a lot of help on the Internet, and you need to take one step at a time toward getting your paper done. Just tell yourself, "I will get this done! I will get this done! I will get this done!"—just like the little engine who could.

**The second thing *not* to do is wait until the last minute to begin your paper.** Sometimes students think if they just wait and put the assigned paper out of mind, it will go away, or something magical will happen to cause an "A" paper to fall into their hands. Maybe they can find a paper already written on the Internet that they can copy and turn in, or maybe they can just find an article to rewrite and turn in as their own. These are all bad ideas, and your teacher will recognize them as plagiarism or cheating.

**Do start thinking about your paper as soon as it's assigned. The questions you should begin thinking about right away are:**

> **What am I going to write about?**

> **Where am I going to learn enough about that to write a paper?**

**Then you need to start doing something about it!**

This is where the Internet can help you. It won't do your paper for you, but it can help you decide what you want to write about. It can help you find the information you need to write your paper. It can tell you where to learn the basics of writing a research paper. And it can tell you how to avoid the pitfall of plagiarism by telling where you got your information and giving credit to the people or organizations from whom you got it.

Let's begin with question number one: **What am I going to write about?**

Maybe you're lucky. You have a burning interest in a certain subject, and this assignment will give you an opportunity to learn more about it. But if that isn't so and you don't have an idea of where to go to get an idea for your paper, this is an excellent site.

Idea Directory: **http://www.researchpaper.com/directory.html**

When you get to this site, scroll to the area you're to write about: art and literature, science, or history, for example. Then scroll to the specific subject, such as literature. Scroll down the questions until you find one that interests you. Click on it and a search engine will take you to articles online about that question. After you decide what you're going to write about, you need to answer this question:

# WRITING A RESEARCH PAPER *(cont.)*

**Where am I going to learn enough about that to write a paper?**
First, you will check the articles you found at the Idea Directory when you looked for an answer. Read those. Note the ones you find interesting and that have to do with the topic you've decided to write about. Note where they are or bookmark the sites so you can come back to them later.

**But before you go any further, you need to learn just what you need to do to write your paper.**
It's easy to take on a bigger job than you will be able to handle, so visit at least one of these sites on writing research papers. The first site, which is at the Purdue Writing Lab, has an easy step-by-step procedure with a checklist you can follow for writing your paper. This is the site on which most of the information in this activity will be based. Try it first, and then if you still feel the need of further help, try the other sites for additional ideas. **Print Purdue's step-by-step procedure.**

Writing Research Papers: **http://owl.english.purdue.edu/Files/94.html**

**Other sites:** At Researchpaper.com, scroll to **Writing Center**, and then **Writing Research Papers & Citing Sources**.

Researchpaper.com: **http://www.researchpaper.com/**

The Research Essay: **http://www.clearcf.uvic.ca/writersguide/Pages/ResearchEssayType.html**

What does the Purdue Writing Lab call "The Preliminaries" of writing a research paper?

1. _____

2. _____

3. _____

4. _____

Now that you know what you're going to write about and you have a good idea about what a good research paper is, you need to **narrow down your topic**, lest you get into that old problem area of "biting off more than you can chew." If your subject is too broad or too general, you will drown in information, lack focus and write a poor paper.

**Write your thesis statement, then focus your study.** Review what a thesis statement consists of one page. From now on, all the research and information-seeking you do will be about what you have just stated is your thesis. You want to focus your energy toward that end. Don't allow yourself to be sidetracked into other subjects, or into things which are not important to this subject. There are many, many interesting things in the world, but you need to take them one at a time. Leave the subjects which aren't relevant to what you're doing here until another time and for another paper. Return to the Purdue step-by-step procedure.

# WRITING A RESEARCH PAPER *(cont.)*

What does it say to do when **gathering data**?

1. _____

2. _____

3. _____

Where should you check in the **library reference room**?

1. _____

2. _____

3. _____

4. _____

In addition to using the library and consulting the reference librarian, you are going to consult the Internet. **Here are some of the Internet resources to which you will go when looking for information.**

> **Sites you've already found through the Idea Directory.**
>
> **Encyclopedia** (list at back of book)
>
> **Search engines** (list at back of book)
>
> **Keywords, if you have that capability through your server**

Remembering that you want to keep your subject limited so you don't spin your wheels collecting data you won't use, begin taking notes. What does Purdue's step-by-step procedure tell you about **taking notes**?

1. _____

2. _____

3. _____

4. _____

Go to a dictionary and find the definition of plagiarism:

**Plagiarism is** _____

_____

# WRITING A RESEARCH PAPER *(cont.)*

You next need to **outline your paper.** An outline is a brief sketch of the main points you want to cover in your research paper. It will give you a "map" of where to go with your paper and help you focus on what to do with your material. The first site will show you two different ways of doing this. The Purdue site will give examples of outlines.

Organizing Your Ideas: **http://members.aol.com/kilvngstn/essay/outline.html**

Developing an Outline: **http://owl.english.purdue.edu/Files/63.html**

Now after all the work you've done, you're finally ready to write your paper. What does Purdue's step-by-step procedure say to do when **writing the paper**?

1. _____

2. _____

    a. _____

    b. _____

3. _____

4. _____

5. _____

6. _____

7. _____

**Revise and rewrite.** This part of writing a paper is one of the most important elements of any good writing. The first draft of a paper is often called a "rough draft" for good reason. In it, you "rough out" what you want to say. You will find you organize your thoughts while writing, and when you go back to your first draft and read it, you will almost certainly notice you still need to tie things together and correct spelling and grammatical errors. Add something here, take something out there.

**Write your paper on a word processor.**

**Check and double-check your sources.** For information on how to list your sources in your bibliography, go to these sites.

How to Cite Electronic Resources: **http://www.williams.edu:803/library/library.www/cite.html**

MLA Citation Examples: **http://www.hcc.hawaii.edu/education/hcc/library/mlahcc.html**

Citing Electronic Sources: **http://owl.english.purdue.edu/Files/110.html**

Office of Learning Resources Web site: **http://doe.state.in.us/LearningResources/**

# BE A SUPER CYBERSPACE EXPLORER

This activity is for the student who has gained some agility on the Internet. A few sites you might use to find the answers to these questions are below, but you may need to do some searching of your own in other places.

**Identify the following people, and note the site from which you got the information:**

1. He had a sword named Excalibur. _____

2. He reportedly chased the snakes from Ireland. _____

3. She told the tales of The Arabian Nights Entertainments. _____

4. A famous oracle gave the name of this town. _____

5. A sword hung by a hair over his head. _____

6. These half-woman, half-bird monsters lured sailors to their deaths on the rocks with their songs.

    _____

7. She was so powerful that anyone who gazed at her turned to stone. _____

8. He had to clean the Augean stables. _____

9. Whose helmet made him invisible?_____

10. Who was a god of fire but became the god of craftsmen? _____

11. Name the seven daughters of Atlas._____

12. Name the winged horse. _____

13. He lived in the labyrinth. _____

14. She turned men into swine. _____

**Bonus points for naming the culture from which each of these come.**

General Folklore and Mythology: **http://pibweb.it.nwu.edu/~pib/mythgene.htm**

Folklore, Myth and Legend: **http://www.acs.ucalgary.ca/~dkbrown/storfolk.html**

Legends Site map: **http://www.legends.dm.net/sitemap.html**

# BE A SUPER CYBERSPACE EXPLORER *(cont.)*

## Who said that?

What did these people say in the given situation?

1. George Mallory when he was asked why he wanted to climb Mt. Everest.

_____

2. Marie Antoinette when she was told her people were hungry.

_____

3. John Paul Jones when he was asked to surrender.

_____

4. W.C. Fields when he was asked how he liked children.

_____

5. Oscar Wilde when he was questioned by U.S. Customs officials.

_____

6. Mark Twain when he heard there had been reports he had died.

_____

7. Liberace when he saw bad reviews by critics about his piano playing.

_____

8. Lincoln when he was talking to McClellan about his failure to fight the enemy.

_____

9. Captain Oates when he went outside to commit suicide.

_____

**Bonus points for providing the date on which each quotation was said.**

Bartlett's Familiar Quotations: **http://www.columbia.edu/acis/bartleby/bartlett/**

Quotation Links: **http://www.starlingtech.com/quotes/links.html**

Proverbs: **http://www.geocities.com/~spanoudi/quote-05.html**

# STRANGE AND WONDERFUL TRIVIA

Go to this site and find the answer to these questions about some very odd words.

Word Oddities and Trivia:  **http://members.aol.com/gulfhigh2/words.html**

1.  What is the only other word in English that ends in -gry besides angry and hungry?

    _____

2.  What is the longest word in common use with no letter appearing more than once?

    _____

3.  What is the longest word whose letters are in alphabetical order?

    _____

4.  What is the longest acronym?

    _____

5.  Name the longest word which has no letter appearing more than once.

    _____

6.  Name three or more words with three letters dotted in a row.

    _____

7.  What word has eight different correct spellings?

    _____

8.  What are they?

    _____

9.  What word has a "W" instead of a vowel?

    _____

10. What small bird has a name with ABC in it?

    _____

11. What word has one letter appearing once, two letters appearing twice, and three letters appearing three times?

    _____

12. Name some plural words that become singular when you add -s.

    _____

# HAVE FUN WITH WORDIES

Words can be fun. Millions of people enjoy all sorts of word puzzles: word searches and crosswords, anagrams and wordies. In "wordies," words and phrases are written in ways which illustrate their meanings. Usually the words that best lend themselves to being made into wordies are idioms. Go to this site to find these wordies. Try to guess what each represents, write them in the spaces below, check your answers, and come up with some of your own.

Wordies on the Web: **http://www.cyg.net/~ddoctor/4cc.html**

| Backward glance | Jack in the box | Calm after the storm |
|---|---|---|
| Period in history | Educated guess | Rob from the rich and give to poor |
| Ring around a rosy | Three little pigs | Mind over matter |
| Feeling under the weather | Tennis anyone? | Three part harmony |
| English sheepdog | Hole in one | Buckle up |

**Now you try** *hole-in-the-wall, in place, on time, off duty, hold off.*

**Can you think of any of your own?**

# HAVE FUN WITH AUTHOR ANAGRAMS

The word "anagrams" was used to indicate words which were spelled backwards, but it has now come to mean words with the letters mixed up. You can read more about anagrams at this first site. The following two sites may be able to help you solve your anagrams. These may be better when solving anagrams with words than they are with anagrams using scrambled names, however. Jumble gives an instant answer. The correct answer may not have the same number of words as the anagram.

Anagrams: **http://www.m-w.com/lighter/name/anagrams.htm**

Andy's Anagram Solver: **http://www.ssynth.co.uk/~gay/anagram.html**

Jumble and Crossword Solver: **http://ull.chemistry.uakron.edu/cbower/jumble.html**

Try to solve these anagrams. All of them are the scrambled names of famous authors.

1. DOLL OCTETS_____

2. LAWYER PENCE_____

3. AN UGLY SPARE_____

4. JULY BUD ME_____

5. NEED ILLEGAL MEN_____

6. GNASH ON THE SLUG_____

7. AWAIM KNIT_____

8. DRAW LEADER_____

9. AN OLD, LARGE APE_____

10. ROBERT'S FORT_____

11. AUTOMATICALLY SO_____

12. I AM WEAK, HELPLESS AIR_____

How many did you get? Now, it's your turn to confound others! Go to this site, type in your name, that of a friend, or anyone else you wish, and within 24 hours you will have a list of anagrams for that name.

Anagram Genius Server: **http://www.genius2000.com/anagram.html**

# LANGUAGE ARTS PUZZLE

## Across

1. story which tells why things are as they are
3. word that takes the place of a noun
5. folk tale
6. action word
7. definition, narrative, or literary
8. person in a story
9. when and where a story takes place
11. someone who writes poems
12. expresses a complete thought

## Down

1. theme of a fable
2. story
3. part of sentence containing verb
4. relating of events
10. person, place, or thing

# WORD GAMES AND ENGAGING SITES

Who doesn't like to play word games and games of all kinds, especially on a Friday or the last day before a holiday break? Here are a number of sites where you can go to play various games. Most of them are word games, although a few are not. A brief description accompanies each link. Be sure to check these out for appropriateness for your students.

1. Word Angst: **http://www.dujour.com/wordangst/**

   This site has a weekly word contest guaranteed to frustrate your brightest students. One meaning clue is given to the word in question, and the student must guess what the word is. The student is only told whether he is right or wrong, so don't send your insecure kids to this one. There are prizes for those accurately guessing the correct word. Hopefully, the site will inspire students to seek out the correct word on their own, but don't count on it! They may just get word angst, indeed, but at least they'll learn a new word! Maybe!

2. The Labyrinth: **http://www.dujour.com/labyrinth/**

   In this game, you must find your way through a series of rooms to the lair of the minotaur. The site includes an account of the myth of the minotaur and would be a good supplementary activity when studying mythology and legends.

3. Mondotrivia: **http://www.dujour.com/mondotrivia/**

   Mondotrivia asks a trivia question such as who the popular actor was who first played the character Molly in *The Unsinkable Molly Brown?* (Answer: Debbie Reynolds) If you guess correctly, your name is entitled to be entered in a drawing for prizes.

4. Riddle du jour: **http://www.dujour.com/riddle/**

   Du jour means word of the day in French, and this site has a new riddle every day for students to try to figure out.

5. Crossword Puzzle Solver: **http://www.eecg.toronto.edu/~bryn/HTML/Crosswords.html**

   Type in the known letters of a word on your crossword puzzle plus the total number of letters to find the answer. You will receive possibilities for your word.

6. NetNoose: **http://people.netscape.com/nathan/netnoose/index.html**

   Play hangman with people all over the world.

7. National Spelling Bee: **http://www.spellingbee.com/**

   Go to this site for information on how to take part in the National Spelling Bee.

8. Aboard Puzzle Depot: **http://www.puzzledepot.com/puzzles.shtml**

   This is a commercial program for creating crossword puzzles for the classroom which you may order at cost. It claims to create crosswords from given list of words in minutes.

9. Jumble and Crossword Solver: **http://www.ull.chemistry.uakron.edu/cbower/jumble.html**

10. Spelling Test: **http://www.sentex.net/~mmcadams/spelling.html**

    Take the spelling test of the fifty most commonly misspelled words to see how you do.

11. Wordies on the Web: **http://www.cyg.net/~ddoctor/4cc.html**

# WORD GAMES AND ENGAGING SITES (cont.)

12. Fake Out!: **http://www.eduplace.com/dictionary/index.html**
    This is a definition guessing game for grades to 6+. Students may also write their own weird definitions to see how many people choose theirs.

13. FroggerSpeller—Sound On: **http://yip5.chem.wfu.edu/yip/shockwave/frog1.html**
    This spelling game is a mix of hangman and Frogger. You unlock the letters by helping the frogs cross the river to dock on the other side. Note: You'll need to have the Shockwave plug-in for your web browser to play. If you do not have the plug-in, go to Macromedia's web site (**http://www.macromedia.com/**) to download Shockwave.

14. Word Oddities: **http://members.aol.com/gulfhigh2/words.html**

15. WebBattleship: **http://gen.ml.org/battle/**
    Note: Your web browser will need to be Java enabled (check preferences in your browser).
    This traditional Battleship game is played online.

16. Checkers: **http://darkfish.com/checkers/Checkers.html**
    Note: Your web browser will need to be Java enabled (check preferences in your browser). This game is not free.
    This traditional checkers game is played online.

17. Desdemona: Interactive Othello: **http://www.math.hmc.edu/~dmazzoni/cgi-bin/desmain.cgi**
    Find at this site an online edition of Othello.

18. Joseph Wu's Origami Page: **http://www.origami.vancouver.bc.ca/**
    Learn to create all sorts of things with paper by using traditional Japanese techniques.

19. Castles on the Web: **http://fox.nstn.ca/~tmonk/castle/castle.html**
    Find pictures and histories of all the world's famous castles.

20. Girls Tech: **http://www.girltech.com/index.html**
    Although intended just for girls, many parts of this site would be interesting to boys as well. It has a teacher resource page and activity book with vocabulary activities such as palindromes, science games, and math games to play online or print and play offline. It includes concentration, story starters, crazy story maker, pig Latin, and scavenger hunt. At the Girls Tech story starters, for example, at **http://www.girltech.com/HTMLworksheets/GC_story_starters.html** the student is given a setting with time and place, a character and specific actions. The students then write a story with what they're given and send it to GT. At the pig Latin site, they type in a message which is translated into pig Latin for them.

# SEND GREETING CARDS

One of the great advantages of the Internet is that you can send a greeting to a friend or loved one any time without having to go to the store to buy an expensive card and without having to remember to buy stamps. There are many sources where you can obtain these cards, and the sites here are just a few of them.

Some cards are beautiful and serious, others funny or silly. You can even send animated greeting cards, holiday cards or special occasion cards, virtual flowers or virtual gifts, most of them free. Of course, the person you're sending them to has to have a computer and be online to receive them, and you must know his/her correct screen name. Using these greeting card sites, send greetings in the following situations. **Not all greeting card sites are free, so if you use one other than these, be aware there may be a charge.**

When you get to a greeting card site, you will be asked to change the greeting given, use it as it is, or personalize it for the person to whom you're sending it. Usually you will be given enough space to write up to fifty words in your personal greeting. You will also be given a choice of pictures, drawings, or animations from which to choose. For this activity, you will change it according to the directions given here.

Blue Mountain Arts' Electronic Greeting Cards: **http://www.bluemountain.com/**

The Digital Postcard: **http://www.all-yours.net/postcard/**

Electric postcards: **http://www.xenus.com/postcard/**

Free Internet Greeting Cards: **http://www.surme.com/cgc/nonframe.shtml**

Cardmaster: **http://www.cardmaster.com/**

Holiday Greetings by Awesome: **http://www.marlo.com/holiday.htm**

1. **Wish your mother or guardian a happy Mother's Day.** Write an acrostic poem for your mother or guardian on your word processor:

   M _____

   O _____

   T _____

   H _____

   E _____

   R _____

On each line, write something nice about your mother or guardian which begins with the letter given. When you finish your poem, copy it and go to the greeting card site. At the site, paste your poem into the space given for a personal message, change the message given in the way you wish to do so to personalize it. Type your name and screen name in the box for sender and the name and screen name of the person to whom you're sending the card in the box for recipient. Preview the card, and send it. Be sure to include the full screen names, including servers' names, because the card will not go out if you don't.

# SEND GREETING CARDS *(cont.)*

2. **Send your best friend a happy birthday card.** Write a poem for your friend of four lines or more on your word processor. Make it silly or loving, whatever will be appropriate for the relationship you have with each other. Copy the poem and go to the greeting card site. Paste the poem in the space provided for a personal greeting and change the greeting already provided on the card, if you wish. Pick out a picture, cartoon, or animation for your card. Some greeting card sites ask you to also pick out a background, so do that if it's asked for. Type your name and screen name in the box for sender and the name and screen name of the person to whom you're sending the card in the box for recipient. Preview the card and send it. Be sure to include the full screen names, including servers' names, because it will not be sent if you don't.

3. **Send a special holiday card.** There is at least one card site which specializes in holiday cards of all kinds, including Valentine's Day, New Year's, Christmas, and Passover. Use that service or another one. Write a special note to the person who will receive the card. Use your best writing, double-check what you have written for spelling and punctuation errors and then copy it. Go to the card site, paste your note in the message box, and personalize the message already given. Pick out the card style you wish, and if you are to include music, choose that. Type your name and screen name in the box for sender and the name and screen name of the person to whom you're sending the card in the box for recipient. Be sure to include the full screen names, including servers' names, because the card will not go out if you don't. Preview the card and send it.

4. **Send a thank you card.** It's always courteous to thank someone who has done you a favor or given you something nice. Write a thank you note on the word processor which expresses your gratitude for the nice thing done for you or given you by someone. Check your writing for spelling and punctuation errors and then copy it. Go to the card site and choose the picture and style card you wish, something the person to whom you are sending the note would like. Paste your note in the message and personalize the message already given. Type your name and screen name in the box for sender, and the name and screen name of the person to whom you're sending the card in the box for recipient. Be sure to include the full screen names, including server's names, because the card will not go out if you don't. Preview the card, and send it.

**Note:** When you click send to send your card on its way, a screen will come up warning you that this message may be going out and be seen by someone other than the one to whom you are sending it. Just click send or okay, and it will go.

# BIBLIOGRAPHY

Butler, Mark. *How to Use the Internet.* Ziff-Davis Press, 1994.

Clark, David. *Student's Guide to the Internet.* Alpha Books, 1995.

Crumlish, Christin. *The Internet Dictionary—The Essential Guide to Netspeak.* Sbyex, Inc., 1995.

Fraase, Michael. *The Mac Internet Tour Guide—Cruising the Internet the Easy Way and The Windows Internet Tour Guide—Cruising the Internet the Easy Way.* Ventana Press, 1995.

Giagnocavo, Gregory, Time McLain, and Vince DiStefano. *Educator's Internet Companion.* Wentworth Worldwide Media, Inc., 1995.

Gardner, Paul. *Internet for Teachers and Parents.* Teacher Created Materials, Inc., 1996.

Haag, Tim. *Internet for Kids.* Teacher Created Materials, 1996.

Harris, Judi. *Way of the Ferret—Finding and Using Educational Resources on the Internet.* ISTE, 1995.

James, Phil. *Netscape Navigator 2.0 book; The Definitive Guide to the World's Most Popular Internet Navigator.* Ventana Communications Group, 1996.

Leshin, Cynthia B. *Internet Adventures—Step-by-Step Guide for Finding and Using Educational Resources.* XPLORA Publishing, 1995.

Lichty, Tom. *The Official America Online for the Macintosh Tour: 2nd Edition.* Ventana Press, 1994.

McLain, Tim and Vince DiStefano. *Educator's Worldwide Web Tour Guide.* Wentworth World-Wide Media, Inc., 1995.

Miller, Elizabeth, B. The *Internet Resource Directory for K-12 Teachers and Librarians.* Libraries Unlimited, Inc., 1996.

Periera, Linda. C*omputers Don't Byte.* Teacher Created Materials, 1996.

Polly, Jean Armour. *The Internet Kids Yellow Pages.* Osborne McGraw-Hill, Inc., 1996

Sachs, David and Henry Stair. *Instant Internet with WebSurfer.* Prentice Hall, 1995.

Williams, Brad. *The Internet for Teachers.* IDG Books Worldwide, 1995.

# LANGUAGE ARTS INTERNET SITES

## Fun Sites/Greeting Cards

Education Cartoons for teachers:
**http://www.borg.com/~rigtoons/edu.html**

Electric postcards:
**http://www.xenus.com/postcard/**

Toonograms:
**http://www.toonogram.com/glasbergen/**

Laugh Riot Rumor Pages:
**http://starcreations.com/abstract/laughriot/lr-hum02.htm**

Free Internet Greeting Cards:
**http://www.surfme.com/cgc/nonframe.shtml**

Blue Mountain Arts Electronic Greeting Cards:
**http://www.bluemountain.com/**

## Dictionaries:

One-Look Dictionaries:
**http://www.onelook.com/**

Online Symbolism Dictionary:
**http://www.umich.edu/~umfandsf/symbolismproject/symbolism.html/**

Oxford English dictionary:
**http://www.oed.com/**

Roget's Internet Thesaurus:
**http://www.thesaurus.com/thesaurus/**

WWWebster Dictionary:
**http://www.m-w.com/dictionary**

Merriam-Webster's Words From the Lighter Side:
**http://www.m-w.com/lwftw/wftw.htm**

Wordsmith:
**http://www.wordsmith.org/awad/wordlist.html**

# LANGUAGE ARTS INTERNET SITES (cont.)

ShakespeareGlossary:
**http://www.ex.ac.uk/~Pellison/revels/gloss/intro.html**

Visual Thesaurus:
**http://www.plumbdesign.com/thesaurus/**

## Encyclopedia

Encarta Online Home Encyclopedia:
**http://encarta.ms.ncom/EncartaHome.asp**

Encyclopedia.com from Electric Library:
**http://www.encyclopedia.com**

Free Internet Encyclopedia-Micro Reference:
**http://www.cs.uh.edu/%7eclifton/micro.a.html**

Grolier Multimedia Encyclopedia Online:
**http://gme.grolier.com (Subscription service)**

## Mythology, Folklore, and Legend

Ancient Gods (family tree):
**http://www.hol.gr/greece/ancgods.htm**

Hellenic Pantheon:
**http://www.geocities.com/Athens/Acropolis/3628/index.html**

Perseus Project:
**http://www.perseus.tufts.edu/**

Ancient Gods (The Olympians):
**http://www.hol.gr/greece/olymp.htm**

Animals, Myths & Legends:
**http://www.ozemail.com.au/~oban/index.html**

Aesop's Fables:
**gopher://spinaltap.micro.umn.edu/11/Ebooks/By%20Title/aesop**

# LANGUAGE ARTS INTERNET SITES (cont.)

Aesop's Fables Online Collection:
**http://www.pacificnet.net/~johnr/aesop/**

Folklore, Myth, and Legend:
**http://www.acs.ucalgary.ca/~dkbrown/storfolk.html**

Myths and Legends:
**http://pubpages.unh.edu/~cbsiren/myth.html**

General Folklore and Mythology:
**http://pibweb.it.nwu.edu/~pib/mythgene.htm**

Folklore and Mythology Electronic Texts:
**http://www.pitt.edu/%7Edash/folktexts.html**

## Grammar and Writing Sites

Character Analysis:
**http://members. Aol.com/AACTchAndy/edu/charanaly.html**

Guide to Grammar and Writing:
**http://webster.commnet.edu/HP/pages/darling/grammar.htm**

HyperGrammar:
**http://www.uottawa.ca/academic/arts/writcent/hypergrammar/**

Review Parts of the Sentence:
**http://www.uottawa.ca/academic/arts/writcent/hypergrammar/rvsentpt.htm**

Owl Handouts:
**http://owl.english.purdue.edu/writers/by-topic.html**

5-Paragraph Essay:
**http://members.aol.com/AACTchAndy/edu/essayform.html**

Basic Guide to Essay Writing:
**http://members.aol.com/lklingstn/essay/**

Online English Grammar:
**http://www.edunet.com/english/grammar/**

Punctuation:
**http://www.uottawa.ca/academic/arts/writcent/hypergrammar/punct.html**

# LANGUAGE ARTS INTERNET SITES (cont.)

Punctuation Exercises:
**http://owl.english.purdue.edu/Files/17.html**

Essay Builder:
**http://www.2.actden.com/writ_den/tips/essay/index.htm**

LEO Write Place Catalog:
**http://leo.stcould.msus.edu/catalogue.html**

Paradigm Writing Assistant:
**http://www.idbsu.edu/english/cguilfor/paradigm/**

Purdue Online Writing Lab:
**http://owl.english.purdue.edu/**

Sentence Craft:
**http://humanitas.ucsb.edu/users/behrens/cid/tc.htm**

## Literature Sites

Short Fiction:
**http://english-server.hss.cmu.edu/fiction/short.nclk**

Classic Short Stories:
**http://www.bnl.com/shorts/**

English Server Novels online:
**http://english-server.hss.cmu.edu/fiction/novel.nclk**

## Exhibits Collection—Literature

What Makes a Good Short Story:
**http://www..learner.org/exhibits/literature/**

English and Language Room, Links to Authors:
**http://members.aol.com/aac4/private/aachomepage/english/e1/engl102.htm**

Cool Sites for Kids:
**http://www.ala.org/alsc/children.links.html**

IPL Youth Division Author Page:
**http://www.ipl.org/youth/AskAuthor/AuthorLinks.html**

# LANGUAGE ARTS INTERNET SITES (cont.)

Author Webliography:
**http://www.lib.lsu.edu/hum/authors.html**

Books online Authors:
**http://www.cs.cmu.edu/bookauthors.html**

Young Adult Reading (Search):
**http://www.spruceridge.com/reading/**

Irish Literature, Mythology and Folklore:
**http://www.luminarium.org/mythology/ireland/**

Literature Links:
**http://members.tripod.com/~JeanneAnn/literary-links.html**

VOS English Literature Page:
**http://humanitas.ucsb.edu/shuttle/english.html**

Great Writers:
**http://www.xs4all.nl/~pwessel/writers.html**

## Poetry Sites

Poetry Pals Forms and Examples:
**http://www.geocities.com/Enchanted Forest/5165/poetry_samples.html**

Haiku—Creative Writing for Kids:
**http://kidswriting.miningco.com/library/weekly/aa100297.htm**

Cinquains and Diamantes:
**http://kidswriting.miningco.com/library/weekly/aa112097.htm**

Complete Collection of Poems by Poe:
**http://www.rit.edu/~exb1874/mine/poe/poe_ind.html**

Index of Linked Poems:
**http://www.wmich.edu/english/tchg/lit/pms/index.html**

Index of Poets Online:
**http://libarary.utoronto.ca/www/utel/rp/indexauthors.html**

Nonsense Links:
**http://www.2.pair.com/mgraz/Lear/ll.html**

# LANGUAGE ARTS INTERNET SITES (cont.)

Poems:

**http://www.well.com/user/eob/poetry.html**

CMU Poetry Index.

**http://eng.hss.cmu.edu/poetry/**

Poetry for Children:

**http://falcon.jmu.edu/~ramseyil/poechild.htm**

Poetry for Kids:

**http://www.nesbitt.com/poetry/poems.html**

Poetry on the Web:

**http://www.bham.wednet.edu/poetry.htm**

Red Frog Poems from Planet Earth:

**http://redfrog.norconnect.no/~poems/**

Shel Silverstein:

**http://falcon.jmu.edu/~ramseyil/silverstein.htm**

## Quotations Sites

Reference:

**http://galaxy.tradewave.com/galaxy/Reference/Quotations.html**

Bartlett's Familiar Quotations:

**http://www.columbia.edu/acis/bartleby/bartlett/**

Quotation Links:

**http://www.starlingrtech.com/quotes/links.html**

Good Quotations by Famous People:

**http://www.cs.virginia.edu/~robins/quotes.html**

## Shakespeare Sites:

Complete Works of Shakespeare:

**http://the-tech.mit.edu/Shakespeare/works.html**

Shakespeare Site map:

**http://daphne.palomar.edu/shakespeare/sitemap.htm**

# LANGUAGE ARTS INTERNET SITES (cont.)

Shakespeare, William:
**http://www.encyclopedia.com/articles/11766.html**

Shakespeare's Globe:
**http://www.reading.ac.uk/globe/Globe.html**

Shakespeare Glossary:
**http://www.ex.ac.uk/~Pellison/revels/gloss/intro.html**

Selected Shakespearean Plays:
**http://www.spinne.com/shakespeare/**

The Shakespeare classroom:
**http://www.jetlink.net/~massij/shakes/**

## Biography Sites

Biographies:
**http://members.aol.com/AACTchrOz/biosculture.html**

Biography.com/find:
**http://www.biography.com/find/find.html**

WIC Biography Index:
**http://www.wic.org/bio/index_bio.htm**

Women in American History:
**http://women.eb.com./women/ind_articles.html**

People in Science:
**http://www.windows.umich.edu/people/people.html**

## Citing Sources:

How to Cite Electronic Resources:
**http://www.williams.edu:803/library/library.www/cite.html**

MLA Citation Examples:
**http://www.hcc.hawaii.edu/education/hcc/library/mlahcc.html**

Citing Electronic Sources:
**http://owl.english.purdue.edu/Files/110.html**

# LANGUAGE ARTS INTERNET SITES (cont.)

## Publishing Sites:

For Young Writers:
**http://www.inkspot.com/young/**

Animals, Myths & Legends:
**http://www.ozemail.com.au/~oban/index.html**

KidPub:
**http://www.bir.bham.wednet.edu/wws/wws.htm**

Writing Contests on the Web:
**http://kidswriting.miningco.com/library/blank/msub40.htm**

7-9 Book Nook:
**http://I-site.on.ca/booknook.html**

## Lesson Plans/Teaching

SCORE Language Arts:
**http://www.sdcoe.k12.ca.us/score/cla.html**

CEC Lesson Plans:
**http://www.col-ed.org/cur/**

SCORE Lit CyberGuides:
**http://www.sdcoe.k12.ca.us/score/cyberguide.html**

AskERIC Lesson Plans:
**http://ericir.syr.edu/Virtual/Lessons/**

Awesome Library k-12 Lesson Plans:
**http://www.neat-schoolhouse.org/lesson.html**

Education World:
**http://www.education-world.com/**

Educator's Toolkit:
**http://marlo.eagle.ca/~matink/**

English Teacher.com Search:
**http://www.englishteacher.com/pages/search.htm**

# ANSWER KEY

**p. 16 Online Dictionary Practice:**

1. Merriam-Webster's or Oxford
2. Shakespeare Glossary
3. Roget's Thesaurus
4. M-W Words from the Lighter Side
5. One-Look Dictionaries
6. Online Symbolism Dictionary

**p. 18 Dictionary Practice Weird Words:**

1. One learning the rudiments of something (the abc's)
2. to adorn with or form into mosaic
3. howl or wail
4. anything hollow, a pit, small opening, vacancy
5. an opening, open space, gap, cleft or chasm
6. neck of land between two seas
7. collect in a mass, form into a ball
8. man-eating
9. shaped like a hoof
10. science or study of seals
11. fluent; flowing sweetly or smoothly
12. loud, clamorous, vociferous
13. to cleanse, purify, cleanse
14. with a single hair
15. rough, bristly, shaggy
16. loss of hair
17. fear of going out into crowds
18. puzzle

**p. 19 Word-a-Day:**

1. abolish or annul formally
2. love of books
3. winged staff carried by the god Mercury
4. related by blood
5. scattering of Jews or other group of people from their homeland
6. carelessly or partially dressed
7. like Falstaff-fat, jovial, and unscrupulous
8. plant or animal living near the ground, or person standing while watching a play
9. clothing
10. hairy, shaggy
11. untiring
12. writing or speech with nonsensical words
13. good-humored
14. mournful, tearful
15. tiny, like the people in Lilliputia
16. placing political expediency above morality characterized by unscrupulous cunning, deception, or expediency
17. given to strict military discipline
18. pretentious like Dickens' character Mr. Micawber
19. self-absorption
20. believing in many gods

Origin in literature: caduceus (mythology); diaspora (Bible); falstaffian (Shakespeare's Henry IV and Merry Wives of Windsor); groundling (referred to in connection with Shakespeare's theatre); jabberwocky (Lewis Carroll, Alice Through the Looking Glass); Lilliputian (Jonathon Swift's Gulliver's Travels); machiavellian (The Prince); micawber (Dickens' David Copperfield); narcissism (mythology)

**p. 25 Literary Periods and Authors:**

*Romanticism:* Characteristics include emphasis on imagination, emotion, introspection, nature; Authors include Rousseau, Goethe, Wordsworth, Coleridge, von Schiller, Lord Byron, Shelley, Keats, Pushkin, Hawthorne, Poe; *Naturalism:* Characteristics based on belief that life follows certain naturally pre-determined patterns and describes minute details of biology and behavior; Authors include Jack London, Frank Norris, Zola, Sherwood Anderson, Dos Passos, Dreiser, deMaupassant, Lbsen, Gorky, Stephan Crane; *Transcendentalism:* Characteristics emphasizes intuitive and spiritual rather than rational or scientific; Authors include Plato, Kant, Emerson, Alcott, Margaret Fuller, Thoreau; *Realism:* Characteristics: familiar aspects of life presented in plain, straight-forward manner; Authors include O'Neill, deBalzac, Flaubert, Tolstoi, Dostoevsky, Chekhov, Eliot, Henry James, Howells, Sinclair Lewis, Auchincloss; *Victorian:* Characteristics prudish and conventional, written between 1840 and 1900; Authors include: Wilde, Eliot, Dickens, Thackeray, Trollope, Carlyle, Ruskin, Tennyson, Rosetti, Swinburne, Stevenson, Hardy.

# ANSWER KEY (cont.)

**p. 28 Idioms: Weird Words and Phrases:**

1. small amount
2. most
3. enough money to pay for
4. I can't even guess
5. there's no limit
6. nervous, apprehensive
7. in trouble
8. to be uncomfortable to be around
9. unaware
10. to evade the subject
12. to first tell about something
13. quit
14. gossip or talk

**p. 32 Gods' Family Tree**

Missing—Chaos, Eros, Hestia, Hades, Poseidon, Hera, Demeter, Athena, Ares, Hephaestus, Persphone, Apollo, Artemis, Atlas, Prometheus, Hermes, Aphrodite.

**p. 35 Symbolism**

*Symbol:* something which represents something else; *ships:* mother, journey, crossing, adventure, *exploration;* **flowers:** young life, sun, childhood, beauty; *birds:* human desire to fly, to become an angel, imagination, freedom, the soul; *butterflies:* transformation, hope, rebirth, resurrection, triumph of the spirit; *serpents:* death, destruction, evil, temptation, the devil, deceit; *mountains:* nearness of God, sky, heavens, permanence; *spiders:* excessive ambition, anguish, narcissism, weavers; *eagles:* sun, inspiration, victory, pride, royalty, power.

**p. 38 Literary Terms Puzzle**

1. main character
2. protagonist
3. antagonist
4. hero
5. plot
6. climax
7. characters
8. setting
9. resolution
10. author
11. rising action
12. narrator

**p. 38 Bonus points:**

2. Atticus
3. Mr. Cunningham
7. Scout, Jem, Atticus, Dill, Calpurnia, and others
8. the South during the 1930's
10. Harper Lee
12. Scout

**p. 42 Shakespeare Scavenger Hunt:**

1. Mary Arden
2. Hathaway
3. Susanna, Judith, Hamnet
4. Globe
5. Thames
6. Tower of London
7. Titus Andronicus
8. Accept any two of dagger, rapier, sword, crossbow, mace, spear, pike, halberd, bill, partisan, arquebus, dag, bird bow
9. 1564
10. Romeo and Juliet
11. Hamlet
12. accept any comedy
13. accept any tragedy
14. accept any history
15. by number

**p. 43 Shakespeare Quotations:**

1. Hamlet
2. Richard III
3. Romeo and Juliet
4. Romeo and Juliet
5. Henry V
6. Merry Wives of Windsor
7. Hamlet
8. Henry IV, Part II
9. Othello
10. As You Like It
11. Julius Caesar
12. Cymbeline

# ANSWER KEY (cont.)

**p. 50 Finding Themes:**

1. moral
2. teaching
3. its view of life and how people behave
4. accept any reasonable answer
5. its theme
6. accept any reasonable answer

**p. 51 Writing Book Reviews:**

1. plot, characters, setting
2. tell how you like it
3. author, title, publishing information, type of book, theme, maybe background
4. give brief overview
5. briefly tell story line
6. describe, respond; explore, relate your argument; relate book to larger issues
7. reasons why

**p. 56 Prepositional Phrases:**

1. nouns, pronouns and phrases to other words in a sentence
2. when, where, why or how
3. accept any reasonable answer
4. the noun phrase
5. a preposition, its object and any associated adjectives or adverbs

**p. 57–58 Grammar Treasure Hunt:**

1. nouns, verbs, adjectives, adverbs, pronouns, prepositions, conjunctions, and interjections
2. part of a sentence
3. a claus which can stand alone as a sentence
4. accept any reasonable answer
5. no noun-verb agreement
6. by adding -s
7. pronouns take the place of nouns, antecendents are nouns to which pronouns refer
8. when a verb's action takes place
9. It cannot stand alone as a sentence
10. accept any reasonable answer
11. accept any reasonable answer
12. accept any reasonable answer
13. accept any reasonable answer
14. a subject and a predicate
15. girl's, children's, woman's, fox's, goat's

16. Turn the verb into a question by asking "whom?" or "what?" after it
17. connects a subject to a subject complement
18. a noun or adjective which refers to the subject. Example: Mary is a stewardess. "Stewardess" is a complement which tells what Mary is.

**p. 61 Jabberwocky:**

<u>Twas</u> <u>brillig</u>, and the slithy <u>toves</u>

<u>Did</u> <u>gyre</u> and <u>gimble</u> in the wabe;

All mimsy <u>were</u> the <u>borogoves</u>,

And the mome raths outgrabe.

<u>Beware</u> the <u>Jabberwock</u>, my <u>son</u>!

The <u>jaws</u> that <u>bite</u>, the <u>claws</u> that <u>catch</u>!

<u>Beware</u> the Jubjub <u>bird</u>, and <u>shun</u>

The frumious <u>Bandersnatch</u>!"

He <u>took</u> his vorpal <u>sword</u> in hand:

Long time the manxome <u>foe</u> he <u>sought</u> —

So <u>rested</u> he by the Tumtum <u>tree</u>,

And <u>stood</u> awhile in <u>thought</u>.

And as in uffish <u>thought</u> he <u>stood</u>,

The <u>Jabberwock</u>, with <u>eyes</u> of <u>flame</u>,

<u>Came</u> <u>whiffling</u> through the tulgey <u>wood</u>,

And <u>burbled</u> as it <u>came</u>!

One, two! One, two! And through and through

The vorpal <u>blade</u> <u>went</u> snicker-snack!

He <u>left</u> it dead, and with its <u>head</u>

He <u>went</u> <u>galumphing</u> back.

And <u>has</u> thou <u>slain</u> the <u>Jabberwock</u>?

<u>Come</u> to my <u>arms</u>, my beamish <u>boy</u>!

O frabjous <u>day</u>! Callooh! Callay!

He <u>chortled</u> in his joy.

<u>Twas</u> brillig, and the slithy <u>toves</u>

<u>Did</u> <u>gyre</u> and <u>gimble</u> in the <u>wabe</u>;

All mimsy <u>were</u> the <u>borogoves</u>,

And the mmorne <u>raths</u> outgrabe.

# ANSWER KEY *(cont.)*

**What the White Rabbit Said:**

They <u>told</u> me you <u>had been</u> to her,
And <u>mentioned</u> me to him:
She <u>gave</u> me a good <u>character,</u>
But <u>said</u> I <u>could</u> not <u>swim.</u>
He <u>sent</u> them <u>word</u> I <u>had</u> not <u>gone</u>
(We <u>know</u> it <u>to be</u> true):
If she <u>should push</u> the <u>matter</u> on,
What <u>would become</u> of you?
I <u>gave</u> her one, they <u>gave</u> him two,
You <u>gave</u> us three or more;
They all <u>returned</u> from him to you,
Though they <u>were</u> mine before.
If I or she <u>should chance to be</u>
<u>Involved</u> in this <u>affair,</u>
He <u>trusts</u> to you <u>to set</u> them free,
Exactly as we <u>were.</u>
My <u>notion</u> <u>was</u> that you <u>had been</u>
(Before she <u>had</u> this fit)
An <u>obstacle</u> that <u>came</u> between
Him, and ourselves, and it.
Don't <u>let</u> him <u>know</u> she <u>liked</u> them best,
For this <u>must</u> ever <u>be</u>
A <u>secret,</u> <u>kept</u> from all the <u>rest,</u>
Between yourself and me.

**p. 62 Writing Sentences:**

1. subject and predicate
2. find the verb
3. an order or command
4. never
5. noun or pronoun
6. verbs
7. stand alone
8. is a group of independent clauses not connected with conjunctions
9. has a subject and predicate and can stand alone
10. has a subject and predicate but cannot stand alone
11. yes
12. no

**p. 63 Identifying Sentences:**

1. Dep
2. R-O
3. FS
4. CX
5. SS, Ind
6. CP
7. Ind, SS
8. Dep
9. CP
10. CP

**p. 66 Writing Paragraphs:**

1. topic sentence
2. the main idea of the paragraph
3. supporting sentences
4. facts, details, examples
5. the main idea
6. when you organize your ideas
7. You turn your ideas into sentences;
8.
   a. check spelling
   b. check grammar
   c. read paragraph
   d. Make sure each sentence has a subject
   e. See if subjects and verbs agree
   f. check verb tenses
   g. Make sure each sentence makes sense
9. definition, classification, description, compare and contrast, sequence, choice, explanation, evaluation

**p. 84 Poetic Terms:**

1. comparison using as or like
2. identified with something else
3. repetition of consonant sounds
4. story told in song
5. unrhymed iambic pentameter
6. long narrative poem
7. lines of iambic pentameter that rhyme in pairs
9. organized into regular speech patterns
10. figurative language evoking the senses

# ANSWER KEY (cont.)

11. words that sound like what they denote
12. long lyric poem usually praising person or thing
13. in a work good is rewarded, evil punished
14. ending syllables in similar sound
15. fourteen line lyric poem of one stanza, iambic pentameter

## p. 86 Figurative Language in Poetry:

1. the Negro
2. the Negro people
3. because they've lived on earth longer than anyone else
4. accept any reasonable answer
5. accept any reasonable answer

## p. 87 Symbols in Poetry:

1. hope, renewal
2. fate, travel through unknown
3. young life, sun, star
4. mystery, testing, secret-filled place through which man must travel to find meaning
5. chaos, opposite of light
6. divine intervention, elusiveness
7. freedom

## p. 104 What is an essay?

1. defines and explains a subject
2. criticizes or defends a subject
3. communicates what you feel or think about a subject
4. tells a story
5. tells how two or more things are alike and different
6. breaks a large subject down into simpler categories and analyzes them
7. discusses a piece of literature or a topic concerned with literature
8. essay written in class in response to a question

## p. 106 Writing a Thesis Statement:

1. states an assertion
2. takes a stand
3. states the main idea
4. narrows the topic
5. makes one main point
6. does not state a fact or observation
7. does not announce a subject
8. does not serve as a title
9. does not have more than one point

## p. 107 Write a definition essay:

1. accept any reasonable answer
2. accept any reasonable answer
3. accept any reasonable answer
4. details, examples, incidents, comparisons, saying what it is not, classify it, tell its origin, tell its effects or results

## p. 109 Writing a Comparison/Contrast Essay:

1. Compare, then contrast
2. Do one idea, then do the other
3. Write only about comparable and contrastable elements of each idea
4. Only compare or contrast
5. to structure a paragraph or to work within other techniques

## p. 110 Writing a Narrative Essay:

1. to make a point
2. get so hung up on telling a story you forget to make a point
3. Watchmakers may cause what they try to prevent
4. short, fast-paced words moving from one thing to another quickly
5. Paragraphs are shorter today.

# ANSWER KEY (cont.)

**p. 111 Writing a Literary Essay:**

1. how a character's personality is shown by action, dialogue, thought, or what is said by him or someone else

2. struggle within a story

3. the speaking of characters

4. words which evoke pictures in the reader's mind to show mood, atmosphere, tension

5. vantage point from which the action of a story is shown

6. something which stands for something other than what it is

7. author's attitude toward the subject

**p. 120 Be a Super Cyberspace Explorer:**

1. King Arthur
2. St. Patrick
3. Scheherezade
4. Delphi
5. Damocles
6. sirens
7. Medusa
8. Hercules
9. Perseus
10. Vulcan
11. the Pleiades
12. Pegasus
13. the Minotaur
14. Ceres

**p. 121 Who Said That?**

1. "Because it's there."
2. "Let them eat cake."
3. "I haven't begun to fight."
4. "If they are properly cooked."
5. "I have nothing to declare but my genius."
6. "The reports of my death have been greatly exaggerated."
7. "I cry all the way to the bank."
8. "If you don't want to use the army, I'd like to borrow it for a while."
9. "I am just going outside and may be some time."

**p. 122 Strange and Wonderful Trivia:**

1. anhungry
2. ambidexterously
3. aegilops
4. ADDOMSUBORDCOMPHIBSPAC
5. subdermatoglyphic
6. Beijing, Figi, Hajji, hijinks
7. catercorner
8. catercorner, catercornered, catacorer, cata-cornered, catty-corner, catty-cornered, kitty-corner, and kitty-cornered
9. CWM (a glacial hollow on hillside)
10. Dabchick
11. chincherinchee
12. cares (caress), larges (largess), princes (princess)  The longest one is multimillionaires(s).

**p. 125**

|   |   |   |   |   |   |   |   |   |   |
|---|---|---|---|---|---|---|---|---|---|
| ¹M | Y | ²T | H |   | ³P | R | O | N | O | U | N | ⁴N |
| O |   | A |   |   | R |   |   |   | A |
| R |   | ⁵L | E | G | E | N | D |   | ⁶V | E | R | B |
| A |   | E |   |   | D |   |   |   | R |
| I |   |   |   |   | I |   | ⁷E | S | S | A | Y |
| ⁸C | H | A | R | A | C | T | E | R |   | T |
|   |   |   |   |   | A |   |   |   | I |
|   |   | ⁹S | E | T | T | I | ¹⁰N | G |   | V |
|   |   | E |   |   | O |   | ¹¹P | O | E | T |
|   |   |   |   |   | U |   |   |   |
|   |   | ¹²S | E | N | T | E | N | C | E |